*The **USS IOWA** (BB 61) on sea trials in late March 1945 after her overhaul at Hunter's Point Naval Shipyard. Resplendent in her new Measure 22 camouflage, she is shown here steaming off San Pedro with the flag of Rear Admiral Badger (Commander Battleship Division SEVEN) flying from the mainmast. After a brief training period she sailed for Okinawa via Pearl Harbor and Eniwetok.*

USS IOWA (BB 61)

by Robert F. Sumrall

INTRODUCTION

The **USS IOWA (BB61)** was the lead ship of a class of six fast battleships ordered by the U.S. Navy for service during World War II. Only four were completed and they still exist today. As of the date of this publication the **IOWA (BB61), NEW JERSEY (BB62),** and **MISSOURI (BB63)** are in commission after being extensively modernized. The activation and modernization of the **WISCONSIN (BB64)** is underway and she is scheduled to be commissioned in 1988.

The **IOWAs** are the most powerful battleships built by the United States and many feel that they are the most handsome vessels ever designed. Except for four battleships which are preserved as memorials in the United States, The **IOWAs** are the sole survivors of a great fleet of battleships built by all of the major naval powers around the world.

Rendering by Paul Bender

*The first **IOWA** was a screw sloop of war, first rate, as shown in this artist's rendering. Launched at the Boston Navy Yard in 1864 she was one of the larger ships in the Navy with a length of 335' and displacing 3,850 tons. On speed trials in 1868 she made better than 17 knots and at that time was the fastest ship in the Navy. She became a victim of the sail versus steam controversy and was laid up in ordinary at Boston soon after her speed run. She was sold out of service on 27 September 1883.*

*Launched in 1896, the second **IOWA** (BB 4) was one of our earliest battleships and the newest and most powerful vessel to fight in our war with Spain. She participated in the cruise around the world of the "Great White Fleet" and was last decommissioned in 1919. Sunk as a target, she was stricken from the Navy list 27 March 1923. She is shown here on 3 October 1911 leaving the New York Navy Yard after her military mainmast was replaced with a new cage mainmast.*

Ships Named IOWA

The **USS IOWA (BB61)** is the third ship in the U.S. Navy to bear the name. It honors the state of Iowa which was admitted to the Union in 1846 as the twenty-eighth state.

The first **IOWA** was a screw sloop-of-war built by the Boston Navy Yard and launched 21 July 1864 as the **USS AMMONOOSUC.** She was 335' long, 44' 4" wide, had a 10' 10" mean draft, and displaced 3,850 tons. Her battery was 10, 9-inch smooth bore guns, 3, 60-pound rifled guns, and 2, 24-pound Howitzer guns. Chief Engineer of the Navy, B.F. Isherwood, USN designed the propulsion machinery and during her speed trials in June 1858, she made better than 17 knots. At that time she was the fastest ship in the Navy. Later in 1868 she was laid up in ordinary at Boston never to put to sea again. Her name was changed to **IOWA** on 15 May 1869. The first **IOWA** apparently became a victim of the sail versus steam controversy raging in the Navy after the War Between the States and was stricken from the Navy Register on 27 September 1883 and sold for scrap.

The second **IOWA (BB4),** one of our earliest battleships, was built by Wm. Cramp and Sons Shipbuilding Co. at Philadelphia and launched 28 March 1896. She was 362' 5" long, 72' 3" wide, had a 24' draft, and displaced 11,410 tons. Her armament was 4, 12-inch/35 caliber guns in two twin turrets, 8, 8-inch/35 caliber guns in four twin turrets, 6, 4-inch/40 caliber guns, and 18, 6-pound guns. Commissioned on 16 June 1897, the **IOWA** was the newest and most powerful vessel to fight in our war with Spain. The **IOWA** fired the first shot at the Battle of Santiago de Cuba and distinguished herself in that action. She was decommissioned and recommissioned several times before serving in World War I. Her final decommissioning was on 31 March 1919 at Philadelphia. On 22 March 1923 the **IOWA,** now classed as Coast Battleship No. 4, was sunk as a target. She was stricken from the Navy Register on 27 March 1923.

The next vessel selected to carry the name was **BB53** which was laid down as **IOWA** at Newport News Shipbuilding & Drydock Co. on 17 May 1920. All work on **BB53** was suspended on 8 February 1922 when the ship was 31.8 percent complete. Construction was cancelled on 17 August 1923 in accordance with the terms of the Washington Treaty limiting naval armaments and she was sold for scrap on 8 November 1923.

This drawing room model shows the first **IOWA** (BB 49) class as they would have appeared. They were to mount 12, 16-inch guns for a main battery and were to be capable of 23 knots. None were completed and all were scrapped in accordance with the Washington Treaty.

THE FAST BATTLESHIP

The concept of the fast battleship resulted from the desire to combine the best features of the battleship and battlecruiser. By general definition both types carried the same heavy main battery but differed in regard to speed and protection. In theory, battleships were protected against weapons comparable to their main battery guns by heavy armor plate. On the other hand, battlecruisers were considerably faster but protected by much lighter armor plate. The battlecruiser's speed was intended to compensate, at least in part, for its lighter armor reasoning that a faster moving target would be harder to track and hit. With the rapid improvement in naval gun fire control the speed advantage of the battlecruiser steadily declined against the battleship as an opponent. Both speed and protection equate to weight and it became obvious that a fast battleship would be considerably larger and heavier than either of the existing types.

The **IOWAs** were the first, and indeed the only true, fast battleships built by the U.S. Navy. To understand the reasons for their development, some background in American naval strategy is helpful, if not necessary.

During World War I, the United States was the only major naval power which did not have battlecruisers, and they were considered necessary to counter the tactical situation presented by the countries possessing them.

By the end of the war, the U.S. Navy was in the midst of a huge expansion program. Six 43,200 ton battleships mounting 12, 16-inch guns, and six 43,500 ton battlecruisers carrying 8, 16-inch guns were under construction. The battleships were to be capable of 23 knots, or only a knot or two faster than the ships in the existing battle fleet, but the battlecruisers were to have a top speed of 33.25 knots and clearly were intended to be among the fastest ships afloat.

An artist's rendering of the **LEXINGTON** (CC 1) in her final design configuration as a battlecruiser. The ships of this class were to carry 8, 16-inch guns and to have a speed of 33.25 knots. They would have been the first fast capital ships in the U.S. Navy. The **LEXINGTON** and her sister **SARATOGA** (CC 2) were completed as aircraft carriers and the rest of the class was scrapped to comply with the Washington Treaty.

The Japanese battlecruiser KONGO, shown here at speed in 1937, and her sisters KIRISHIMA, HARUNA AND HIEI could make 26 knots. This speed advantage over the 21 knot U.S. Navy battle line drove the design of all future U.S. capital ships.

The Washington Treaty

In 1921, all of the major naval powers were still continuing their massive building programs, even though the German High Seas Fleet had been dismantled after World War I. Most countries were facing the problems of post-war recession and were unable to finance a naval arms race. In the United States there was little hope that Congress would continue to fund the ambitious building program underway after a costly "war to end all wars." The practical solution was negotiation, the outcome of which was the Washington Treaty of 1922.

The Washington Treaty, which was signed on 6 February 1922 by Great Britain, the United States, Japan, France, and Italy, effected a "building holiday" for ten years. The treaty restrictions were to have a significant effect on U.S. naval strategy and future design.

Total tonnage limitations imposed on the major naval powers were as follows:

Great Britain - 580,450
United States - 500,360
Japan - 301,320
France - 221,170
Italy - 182,000

This establishment was referred to as the "5-5-3" ratio.

Capital ships could not exceed 35,000 tons with a maximum gun size of 16-inches.

The age of a capital ship was determined to be 20 years, and no new replacement was permitted before that time.

Reconstruction of capital ships was permitted, but was limited to improvements against aerial and underwater attack.

Any such improvements were only allowed to increase displacement by 3,000 tons.

The term "standard displacement" was established and defined as the weight of the vessel complete, fully manned, and ready for sea. This includes ammunition, provisions, potable water, and all other items carried in war but excluding fuel and reserve feed water.

Weight was defined as 2,240 pounds per ton (English) and 1,016.05 kilograms (Metric) per ton.

The treaty allowed some new vessels to be completed if they met the treaty restrictions, but most new construction had to be scrapped in order to comply. It was also necessary to dispose of many older vessels to reach the adjusted allotments.

The conference leading to the treaty produced a great amount of wrangling among the signatory powers, but the most bitter disagreement was over the question of total strength allocation. Japan was never satisfied with the "5-5-3" ratio that was established for the top three powers. She felt forced into a position of inferiority and by 1936 had withdrawn from participation in continuing treaty negotiations.

Both the battleship and battlecruiser programs fell victim to the treaty, and all construction underway was cancelled except for the battlecruisers **LEXINGTON** and **SARATOGA.** They were completed as aircraft carriers. As a result of the curtailment of the building program, the existing battle fleet was still only capable of no more than 21 knots. This was not inconsistant with U.S. Navy doctrine at that time for firepower and armor was always advocated over speed. The problem was, as we shall see, that the treaty allowed potential adversaries to retain capital ships with high speed capabilities.

The Probable Enemy

After World War I, our national interest began to focus on the Pacific, and strategic planning was directed toward controlling the sea lanes of this vast ocean. It was assumed that our next war would be with Japan for the domination of the Pacific, and the U.S. Navy began to station major portions of the fleet on the West Coast.

According to the "5-5-3" ratio set by the Washington Treaty, the United States was allowed 15 capital ships and Japan only 9. Of the many battle problems played at the Naval War College it was always expected that the Japanese would try to reduce this advantage by attrition before any confrontation of the battle lines.

Naval strategists assumed that the Philippine Islands, which were our major possession in the Western Pacific, would be the target of any Japanese attack. In the event of such an attack, our forces would be at a disadvantage as they steamed west to relieve the Philippines. To do so, they would have to pass through a chain of islands which had been mandated to the Japanese. The assumption was that the Japanese would fortify these "mandated islands" with a heavy concentration of air and naval bases.

From these bases of operation, Japanese submarines and fast ships such as aircraft carriers and heavy cruisers could attack our advance units and the long lines of communication. The American ships would be struck again as they came within the range of land based aircraft on the Japanese held islands. Once the American treaty advantage was thus sufficiently reduced, the Japanese could then commit their battle line to a decisive engagement.

Three of the capital ships in the Japanese battle line were the 26-knot **KONGO** class battlecruisers **HARUNA, KIRISHIMA,** and **KONGO.** A fourth of the class, the **HIEI,** had been demilitarized and was serving as a training ship. If any of these units were detached from their battle line to assist their carriers and cruisers they would certainly overpower our carriers and cruisers sent out to counter the enemy. Our 21-knot battle fleet could not bring such fast Japanese task groups to action.

Still outraged by the treaty, which they felt was a conspiracy to relegate them to the status of a second class naval power, the Japanese began a modernization and reconstruction program designed to exploit the clauses of the treaty to the fullest. It was their intent to have the finest vessels possible within the agreed limitations and they carefully and deliberately planned how they could extract the maximum fighting capabilities from the vessels which they had.

The **KONGOs,** for instance, were reconstructed twice before Pearl Harbor, and were re-rated as battleships after the second refitting. Secretly, the **HIEI** remilitarized and also modernized bringing her up to the standard of her sister. Another very well kept secret was that the **NAGATO** and **MUTSU,** both mounting eight 16-inch guns, were also capable of 26 knots.

*The French battlecruisers **DUNKERQUE** and **STRASBOURG**, launched in 1932 and 1936, are shown here at anchor in St. Nazaire harbor early in 1939. They were built to counter the three German "pocket battleships" of the **LUTZOW** (ex-**DEUTSCHLAND**) class, the first of which was laid down in 1928. The **DUNKERQUE**s were designed to do 29.5 knots and during their trials were credited with 31.5 knots.*

*An excellent view showing the 11-inch guns of the German battlecruiser **GNEISENAU**, taken in 1939 with her sister the **SCHARNHORST** in the background. It was intended that the tripple 11-inch turrets would be replaced with twin 15-inch turrets. Their speed was rated at 31.5 knots and they were built in reply to the **DUNKERQUE**s.*

The London Treaties

By the late 1920s, the economic situation throughout the world was not conducive to the beginning of another naval armaments race. Yet, in an increasingly paradoxical situation, those countries not at par with Great Britain and the United States wanted equality, even if they couldn't afford it. They saw the possession of giant and powerful floating fortresses as symbolic of their nation's prestige, strength, industrial capability, and scientific achievement.

The Washington Treaty had provided for a conference to be held in London in 1930, a year before the expiration of the "building holiday." In an attempt to assume control of naval arms limitations, the League of Nations called instead for a conference to be held in Geneva in 1927. With the Japanese, French, and Italians nursing their well fermented grievances from the original conference at Washington, the meeting at Geneva was doomed to failure.

The second naval arms limitations conference was duly convened in London in 1930. The same discontent that had ruined the attempt at Geneva shadowed the London talks. By 1930, the Depression had spread throughout the world, and most of the signatory nations were not in a position to spend the funds necessary for capital ship construction at the cost of their nation's economic survival. The state of the world economy was probably the strongest factor in bringing about eventual agreement and the "building holiday" was extended for another five years.

The agreement was not without a price. France refused to ratify, putting forth as justification the fact that Germany had laid down the "pocket battleship" **DEUTSCHLAND** making new ships necessary as a countermeasure.

As expected, Italy also refused to support the treaty, claiming that new French ships would threaten her position in the Mediterranean.

By the time the next naval arms limitations conference was held in London in 1936, a new naval armaments race was well underway. France was building the **DUNKERQUE** class in answer to Germany's "pocket battleships." Italy was countering with a 35,000 ton battleship which turned out to be over 40,000 tons, and Germany responded to France with the **SCHARNHORST** class. The Japanese, meanwhile, had announced that they would no longer participate in any agreement to limit naval arms, claiming the right to build as they considered necessary for their national interests.

Against this gloomy outlook, the remaining signatory countries inserted an "escalator clause" which would allow them parity with those powers not participating in the treaty. It was required, however, that other signatories be consulted before such a move was undertaken. Actually this was only a formality to justify the increase in weight and gun size for new construction.

DESIGN BACKGROUND

Serious design work on new battleships was begun in 1935 and there was no question that an increase in speed was of primary concern. In July of 1935, the General Board[1] asked the Bu C & R (Bureau of Construction and Repair) for design sketches of battleships capable of steaming at 30 knots and armed with either 14 or 16-inch guns.[2] A design was prepared

*Still limited to 35,000 tons the **SOUTH DAKOTA** class represented a major improvement over the **NORTH CAROLINA's**. With a main battery of 9, 16-inch guns, they were somewhat shorter than their predecessors. The weight saved with a shorter hull was allocated to additional protection and machinery, which gave her immunity to 16-inch gunfire and a speed of 27 knots. In this photo, taken 4 June 1942, the **SOUTH DAKOTA** (BB 57) is leaving Philadelphia enroute to the Pacific.*

with nine 14-inch guns, capable of 30 knots, and within the 35,000 ton weight limitation. After some consideration, it was rejected because main battery was considered inadequate. The design was reworked to mount twelve 14-inch guns in three quadruple turrets. The three additional 14-inch guns had their price. In order to stay within the 35,000 ton treaty limit, a three knot reduction in speed had to be accepted. The result was the **NORTH CAROLINA** class.

The **NORTH CAROLINA** was laid down on 3 June 1936 and studies for the next generation of battleships, which would become the **SOUTH DAKOTA** class, were immediately begun. When the Japanese withdrew from participation in the 1936 Treaty, they also refused to state that they would not adopt 16-inch guns in their new designs.[3] As a result, by mid-1937, the U.S. Navy had decided to adapt the 16-inch gun in all new construction and the Bu Ord (Bureau of Ordnance) was asked to design a new triple 16-inch turret for the **NORTH CAROLINA** class. Nine 16-inch guns would replace the twelve 14-inch guns in the new battleships. The next generation designs, now in progress, would also receive the new guns. The U.S. Navy's decision to increase the gun caliber to 16-inch on all new battleships would prove to be a wise one.

A battleship is designed to resist gunfire comparable to its own main battery. In theory, it would overpower a weaker adversary and avoid contact with a more powerful one. When the decision to increase the size of the main battery in the **NORTH CAROLINA** was made, she was already too far along in construction to increase her armor protection. Any increase in armor would have also put her well over the weight limit which was unacceptable.

It was felt that the **NORTH CAROLINA** represented the limit of what could be attained on 35,000 tons and that in some areas she was even badly compromised. Yet the new design, which became the **SOUTH DAKOTA** class was armed with nine 16-inch guns, was protected against them, was capable of 27 knots, and still did not exceed the 35,000 ton limit.

A number of adjustments and accommodations to the **NORTH CAROLINA** design were necessary and, indeed, the key to the success of the new design. First, maximum protection for the least possible weight was achieved by placing the armor belt inboard, inclining it to 19 degrees,

FOOTNOTES

1. The General Board was a group of senior naval officers representing the Office of the Chief of Naval Operations and the Bureaus of Construction and Repair, Engineering, Ordnance, and Navigation. The Board's primary purpose was to determine the mission requirements for each type of vessel and the characteristics necessary to carry out their missions in order to implement national policy.

2. The second London conference would be convened the following year and the somewhat ambiguous instructions reflected the Board's uncertainty concerning the maximum gun caliber that would be allowed.

3. Japan guarded her naval construction program with extreme security measures. After three years of design studies a building plan was approved in March 1937 and the first new battleship that Japan built was laid down at Kure Navy Yard on 4 November 1937. Almost immediately, the shipway was shrouded with huge tarpaulins to prevent observation of design characteristics and building progress. Intelligence reports, however, indicated that the vessel was over 45,000 tons, with 16-inch main armament. Some reports speculated on an even larger vessel armed with 18-inch guns. That vessel was the **YAMATO** and the speculations proved correct.

The keel of the IOWA is "truly and fairly laid" on 27 June 1940 at the New York Navy Yard. Rear Admiral C.H. Woodward, Chief of the Bureau of Construction and Repair, drives the first rivet while yard superintendents, foremen and chargemen look on.

extending it downward, and tapering it to 1 inch at its lower edge. Second, a unique and radically new machinery arrangement was devised with boilers above turbines in the same space. This allowed a considerable reduction in length. Finally, all uptakes were trunked into one funnel and with other topside rearrangements, the superstructure was shortened to be compatible with the spaces below in the hull. These were not easy solutions for they required a great deal of advanced engineering design and development. Although the arrangement was somewhat cramped, the design was viable and proved to be very successful.

Design requirements were finalized in August 1937, and after preparation of contract plans and specifications, the **SOUTH DAKOTA** was laid down on 5 July 1939.

THE IOWA DESIGN

The interest in a fast battleship had by no means abated and the Preliminary Design Section of the Bu C & R conducted various studies of such a vessel after the completion of the **SOUTH DAKOTA** design.

The U.S. Navy had already wisely adopted the 16-inch gun and now it appeared that potential adversaries had actually begun construction of battleships well in excess of the 35,000 ton limit. Intelligence reports of such construction were further fortified by experience with the **NORTH CAROLINA** and **SOUTH DAKOTA** designs. At this point it certainly appeared that the 1936 Treaty signatories would raise the total per ship weight to 45,000 tons.

Early in 1938 the General Board asked for a new study of a fast battleship to determine just what 45,000 tons would buy. The study indicated that an expanded **SOUTH DAKOTA** capable of 33 knots was feasible on the new tonnage. This was the beginning of the **IOWA** class design.

In addition to the 33 knot speed another feature of the new design was a 16-inch/50 caliber gun. This was to have been the main armament for the battleships and battlecruisers cancelled in 1922 and a number of them were available from inventory. This weapon was preferred for its greater range and penetration over the 16-inch/45 caliber installed in the **NORTH CAROLINA** and **SOUTH DAKOTA** classes.

Meanwhile, in March 1938, diplomats from the 1936 Treaty countries were conferring regarding the naval construction programs of non-participants. It was decided to raise the per ship tonnage to 45,000, and in June the treaty was so amended.

The new characteristics were submitted to the General Board 2 June 1938. Ironically, at the same time, the agreement to escalate the treaty was being signed. The Bu C & R was directed to proceed with the contract plans and specifications and the Bu Ord with the design of the new 16-inch/50 caliber turret.

Design proceeded at an accelerated pace and by November 1938 the contract plans were complete. A potentially serious discrepancy was discovered at this point. The turret designed by the Bu Ord did not fit in the space alloted by the Bu C & R hull design. The hull could not be altered without changing its efficiency, which meant a reduction in speed. An alternative would have been a reversion to the 16-inch/45 caliber turret which would easily fit. Neither of these was acceptable. An additional 10,000 tons would have bought very little or nothing at all. The Bu Ord was directed to redesign the turret. They were able to produce a design with a small enough barbette diameter to meet all of the installation requirements of the Bu C & R design.

Originally the General Board had envisioned three fast battleships in reply to the three Japanese **KONGOs** and appropriations for two ships were made in Fiscal Year 1939. These became the **IOWA (BB61)** and **NEW JERSEY (BB62).** The New York Navy Yard was selected to build the lead ship and prepare the working plans for the class. The Philadelphia Navy Yard was awarded construction of the second ship. On 1 July 1939 contracts were signed and New York Navy yard formally began the construction and manufacturing drawings.

*These construction progress photos of the **IOWA** show many design features which will be obscured when the vessel is completed. At right: Construction of the tripple bottom is seen progressing on 30 September 1940. The tunnel stern takes shape aft as the half siding for the keel begins to rise on the plating supports. Below left: Progress as of 4 January 1941 looking forward from about amidships. The boilers are in place in the alternating fire room engine room arrangement. Below center: View looking aft, also taken 4 January 1941. The tunnel stern and twin skegs are taking shape. The torpedo defense system is clearly visible and the armor belt, inclined at 19 degrees, is being hung. Below right: The foundation bulkhead for Turret II is clearly visible in this view looking forward taken 27 June 1941. This structure will be surrounded and protected by the heavy armor of the barbette.*

*At high tide on 27 August 1942 the **USS IOWA** (BB 61) slipped into the East River from her shipway at the New York Navy Yard. Mrs. Henry A. Wallace, wife of the Vice President, christened the vessel named for the home state of the Wallaces. The full shape of the underwater bulb of her distinctive clipper bow is visible. The large external hawse pipe castings are intended to stand off the anchor sufficiently so its flukes will clear the bulb when being raised and lowered.*

*Minutes after launching the **IOWA** comes to a stop in the East River. Tugs have already gathered to tow the huge vessel to a berth in the outfitting basin of the New York Navy Yard where she will be completed and commissioned for service. Note the Elco-built PT 131 in the foreground.*

The design of the **IOWAs** and, in particular their system of armor protection, was predicated on the main battery using the existing 2,240 pound AP shell. In June 1939, the Bu Ord proposed a new 16-inch shell weighing 2,700 pounds to replace the 2,240 pound shell then in use. Although the heavier shell had a lower velocity, it retained its velocity longer and the lower muzzle velocity increased the life and accuracy of the gun. The new shell was adopted. The **IOWA** class was designed to resist the 2,240 pound shell and an increase in armor for protection against the heavier shell was quite impossible on 45,000 tons. (See Armor Protection for the effects on immunity.)

In expanding the **SOUTH DAKOTA** design, the size of the machinery spaces grew considerably to accommodate the increase in horsepower from 130,000 HP to 212,000 HP. The combination engineroom fireroom arrangement created four enormous compartments amidships each 64 feet in length, whereas, in the **SOUTH DAKOTA,** each machinery space was only 40 feet long. A single penetration at one of the main bulkheads would flood 128 feet. The New York Navy Yard proposed an alternating fireroom engineroom arrangement with two boilers in each fireroom and one set of machinery in each engineroom for its propeller shaft. This allowed the four large machinery spaces to be broken up into eight spaces which reduced the flooding from a single hit by half. This also simplified the trunking of the uptakes to the funnels and reduced the size of the penetrations through the armored decks. The new machinery arrangement was ap-

The IOWA conducted her shakedown along the East Coast and in the Chesapeake Bay. She is shown here at anchor off New York on 7 April 1943. Note her clean flowing lines and graceful appearance.

The addition of the gun tub on her bow and other distinctive armament changes were not made until her post-shakedown overhaul.

proved by the Bu C & R and contract plans were revised accordingly. From a damage control and survivability point of view, the delays and expenses incurred were well worth the benefits to be gained from this considerable design change.

The Navy expected to build two more battleships in Fiscal Year 1941, **BB63** and **BB64**. **BB63** was to be a fast battleship but **BB64** was planned as a slower version with possibly 12, 16-inch guns. The War Plans Division now objected, reasoning that they wanted a clear cut superiority in numbers of fast battleships. The General Board finally agreed and on 12 June 1940 the **MISSOURI (BB63)** was ordered from New York Navy Yard and the **WISCONSIN (BB64)** from Philadelphia Navy Yard as fast battleships.

With what it considered a "sufficient number of fast battleships," the General Board ordered studies resumed on the slower, heavier battleships designated **"BB65."** The Congress authorized a large emergency construction program on 19 July 1940 which included two battleships. The General Board wanted these two units to be of the new design, but **"BB65"** was not far enough along and the Secretary of the Navy directed that the two new ships be duplicates of those already designed and under construction. On 9 September 1940 the **ILLINOIS (BB65)** was ordered from Philadelphia Navy Yard and the **KENTUCKY (BB66)** was ordered from Norfolk Navy Yard as units of the **IOWA** class.

General Arrangement

In general, the primary consideration in the design of the **IOWAs** was high speed. Externally, speed meant fine hull lines and extreme length. Internally the same hull lines meant relatively little volume into which barbettes, ammunition, control stations, fuel, supplies, the crew, and 212,000 shaft horsepower could be fitted. The superstructure had to be compact also, so as not to unduly restrict the arcs of fire of the guns and the visibility of the fire control gear. A great deal of the superstructure proper was filled with gun mounts, ammunition hoists, directors, and director tubes, leaving a limited amount of space available for accommodation.

There were three continuous decks: the main or weather deck, which served as the bomb deck; the second deck, which was the principal armored deck; and the third deck, which covered the machinery spaces. A splinter deck was fitted directly below the second, or main armored deck extending from barbette No. 1 to barbette No. 3. The splinter deck was not a full deck height and was placed so close to the second deck that the space between them was not really usable. The lower decks were "platforms," interrupted amidships by the machinery spaces, forming decks forward and aft. From the third deck down were the first, second, and third platform decks. The hold was the next deck below the third platform extending from forward of barbette No. 1 to aft of barbette No. 3 and the flat which carried the foundations for the main machinery. Beneath the

*The **IOWA** is shown in drydock at the New York Navy Yard during her inclining experiment on 28 March 1943. Above right: The gun tubs for the bow 20 mm and the forecastle 40 mm mounts have not yet been added. This clean, uncluttered appearance is reminiscent of pre-war days. Above left: The **IOWA's** original radar suit is clearly visible. Note the three-level conning tower. The upper level contained the MK 40 director and its associated optics can be seen protruding from the top. The middle level was the conning station during battle and the lower level was for observation by the fleet commander. Because of this lower observation level the **IOWA** did not have a 40 mm mount atop Turrett II, as it would have obstructed the view. Three 20 mm mounts would later be added there. The primary conning station is located halfway up the fire control tower. Below right: Looking forward the characteristic shape of the bow is evident. Note the heavy concentration of antiaircraft weapons amidships. Below left: This view shows the arrangement of the aircraft catapults and handling crane. There were no hangar facilities. One OS2U Kingfisher observation plane was stored on each catapult and one was stored on the deck.*

vitals of the ship, the hold formed a triple bottom on top of the double bottom which formed a continuous flat from the stem to aft of barbette No. 3.

There were eight main machinery spaces with an alternating fire room, engine room arrangement located below the third deck and between the conning tower and the after main battery director.

The magazines for the 16-inch guns were located forward and aft of the machinery spaces resting on the inner bottom. The largest part of the

Anchored off the New York Navy Yard on 9 July 1943, the IOWA has just completed her post shakedown overhaul. Note the two 20 mm mounts on the bow and the two 40 mm mounts on the forecastle which have just been added. The open bridge has also had a wind shield installed. Deck Divisions are over the side giving her a final coat of paint.

magazines was allocated to powder stowage. Most of the projectiles were stowed in rings rotating with and hung from the turret mechanism and on shelves supported from the inner sides of the barbette.

The superstructure rose above the main deck in two continuous levels. All of the 10, 5-inch/38 caliber twin gun mounts were concentrated on these two decks designated the 01 and 02 levels. A heavy armored conning tower, from which the slip was commanded in battle, was located near the forward end of the superstructure. The navigating bridge was at the 04 level around the conning tower with the pilot house directly aft. Accommodations for the captain and the flag were below the pilot house.

The primary conning station was at the 08 level on the forward fire control tower. The forward main battery director was located atop the tower with the center of its stereoscopic rangefinder 116' above the waterline.

There were two large funnels, indicative of the ship's massive power plant. The leading edge of the forward funnel was faired into the fire control tower with the flue gases venting from a flat slightly above the primary

A stern view also taken on 9 July 1943. Note the new 40 mm mount on the main deck at the after end of the superstructure. Most of the IOWA's search radar is visible and her IFF system BK ''ski pole'' transponders can be seen on both yardarms. The anchor ball is also visible at the starboard forward yard. The side painters have not as yet worked their way aft.

One of the distinctive looks of the **IOWA** class ships was their narrow clipper bow. Left: The **IOWA** is at anchor off New York on 7 April 1943. When the **IOWA** and the **NEW JERSEY** were first completed, they did not have the 20 mm gun tub on their bows. Note the lighter chain running out of the bull nose which is for streaming paravanes. Below left: The **IOWA** has just completed her post shakedown overhaul at the New York Navy Yard in this 9 July 1943 photo. The 20 mm gun tub has just been added. Below right: This view, also taken 9 July 1943, shows how the gun tub and the 20 mm mounts were installed. The pipes leaning outboard on the forward side of the tub are for cooling 20 mm barrels. The paravane outhaul chain is starboard of the anchor deck bolster. Note how it is led through sheaves to the bull nose.

conning position. The after funnel was free standing and vented slightly lower than the forward one. Large caps were placed on each funnel directing the gases aft. The centers of the uptakes were nearly 100' apart and the primary portion of the 40mm air defense battery was clustered between them.

Aft of the second stack was the after fire control tower with a second main battery director atop. The centerline of its range finder was 68' above the waterline. Weight and stability would not allow the after director to be placed as high as the forward one, therefore, it was placed low enough to avoid most of the gases from the second funnel.

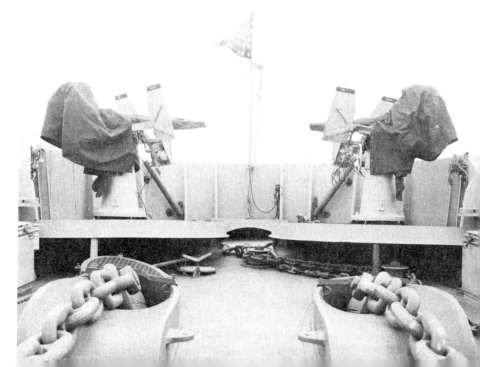

In these photos taken in November 1943 the **IOWA** has just had some modifications made at the Boston Navy Yard. The primary conning station on the fire control tower has been enlarged to include access all around the tower. Additional wind screen protection has also been provided on the top of the pilot house. The top level of the conning tower, which houses the MK 40 director, can be clearly seen. Note the MK 30 and MK 32 periscopes protruding from the top and the MK 3 radar antenna. In the **IOWA** class, the MK 3 radar functionally replaced the MK 9 spotting glass of earlier MK 40 installations, and later was replaced itself by the MK 27 radar.

The **IOWA** makes ready for sea in November 1943 after receiving several modifications at the Boston Navy Yard. She would take President Roosevelt on the first leg of his journey to the Teheran Conference and then return him home. One of the modifications was to build a special bath tub for him in the captain's quarters. The tub still exists today.

These two views show the **IOWA** leaving Hunter's Point Navy Yard on 18 March 1945 after her first major overhaul since she left the East Coast. Her bridge area has been enclosed in a manner similar to that of the **MISSOURI** and **WISCONSIN**. New search and fire control radar is evident and her OS2U Kingfishers have been landed for the later SC-1 Seahawk. Note how the Navy Blue band of her Measure 22 camouflage has been carried up to the sheer line aft.

In the fall of 1946, the **IOWA** was again overhauled, this time at the Puget Sound Navy Yard. She received new SK-2 radar and many of her 20 mm and some 40 mm mounts have been removed. She is now painted Haze Gray on all vertical surfaces but has not yet been given large shaded hull numbers. Note that the paravane downhaul chain is still rigged. These photos were taken on 11 October.

Returning from Korea, the **IOWA** is off Pearl Harbor on her way to the East Coast and Norfolk for an overhaul in this photograph taken 28 November 1952. Her radars include an SPS-6 air search set on her foretop and an SG-6 surface search set on the foretopmast. An SP air intercept is on her maintop and an SG surface search set is on the maintopmast.

The **IOWA** steams off the West Coast early in 1952 just before her first Korean War deployment. Her catapults have been removed and large shaded numbers have been painted on her bow and stern. Note the DBM radar direction finders on the after stack. The fineness of her lines forward show clearly. Her search radar is described with the photograph below.

The **IOWA** is being assisted by tugs at the Philadelphia Naval Shipyard January 1958 where she will be drydocked in preparation for deactivation. Note the quadrapod mainmast supported from the stack and kingposts for the boat handling booms. This was the **IOWA's** final configuration before modernization.

The **IOWA** is eased into drydock at Philadelphia for deactivation. Fuel oil, stores and ammunition have been removed and from the draft marks on the bow she appears to be at a very light load. The **IOWA's** loading is 154 tons per inch immersion. While in drydock the hull, sea chests and appendages will be cleaned, painted and sealed with preservatives.

*The **IOWA** is back in drydock again at Philadelphia in August 1982 being readied for the long tow to Ingalls Shipbuilding at Pascagoula, MS where she will be modernized and recommissioned. The **IOWA** had been exceptionally well preserved by Philadelphia and her material condition was excellent. The vessel seen behind the bow of the **IOWA** is the **WISCONSIN**.*

MODERNIZATION

The **IOWA** served continuously from the time of her first commissioning on 22 February 1943 until she fell victim to post-World War II austerity policies. She was decommissioned on 24 March 1949 and placed in the Atlantic Reserve Fleet at Philadelphia. After the United States was drawn into the Korean conflict in 1950, it became necessary to expand the active fleet and the **IOWA** was recommissioned on 25 August 1951.

After World War II the **IOWA** received the latest radar, electronics and communications suits including a heavier main mast to carry the additional weight of the new equipment. Except for these changes her configuration was nearly identical to that of her wartime service.

In Korean waters, her 16-inch batteries proved invaluable for shore bombardment supporting the ground forces in the seesaw war underway there. After the Korean truce, the **IOWA** remained active until she was again decommissioned and placed in reserve at Philadelphia on 24 February 1958.

During the Vietnam War, the **NEW JERSEY** was activated for a brief time, but none of the other ships in the **IOWA** class were seriously considered for reactivation. As was the case in Korea, the battleship's 16-inch guns provided valuable fire support for the U.S. Marine Corps and Army forces along the coastline.

*In the Reserve Fleet at the Philadelphia Naval Shipyard the **IOWA** rests like a sleeping giant in this view taken 13 August 1974. The vessel to the left, on the **IOWA's** starboard, is the **WISCONSIN**. Most of the radar antennas have been removed and placed in inside storage and all navigating areas such as the bridges have been carefully sealed and preserved.*

In this photo taken in October 1983 the modernization of the IOWA is well underway. All of the rip-out appears to be complete and some of the new structure amidships, which will house the missile batteries and their support equipment, is already in place. The ship is literally blanketed in a maze of scaffolding, power lines, welding leads and air hoses.

The four ships of the **IOWA** class remained in the reserve fleet surviving various attempts at disposal. Surveys during the mid and late 1970's showed them all to be in good material condition with considerable service life remaining. The first serious consideration for reactivation and modernization was in 1980 when the **NEW JERSEY** was included in the FY 81 budget, but she did not survive the budget-cutting process. In a second attempt, she was included in the FY 81 supplemental budget and finally won approval. This was the beginning of the new battleship program which would eventually see all four ships of the **IOWA** class modernized and recommissioned for service in the 600 ship Navy.

The mission of the modernized **IOWAs** is to conduct prompt and sustained combat operations at sea. They are capable of destroying surface, air and shore targets with both guns and missiles and can be projected into a number of roles. In a surface action group a battleship is the principal ship. Its 16-inch guns are unmatched in power and accuracy, and the Harpoon and Tomahawk cruise missiles give her a long range strike capability. The great speed of these ships enables them to combine operations with a carrier battle group forming a sort of super group. They are ideally suited for operating in areas of lesser threat, which enables the more ef-

Work really has just begun on the IOWA's modernization in this 17 July 1983 photo. Plywood sheathing has been laid over the decks to protect the teak decking during construction. The bucklers are being fitted to the guns and can be seen lying atop the turrets together with their expansion tubes and clamping bands. The ship across the pier is a SPRUANCE class destroyer nearing completion.

The IOWA is in the final stages of outfitting at Ingalls Shipbuilding in this photo taken 1 March 1984. Two CG 47 class Aegis cruisers can be seen under construction in the background.

fective deployment of carriers elsewhere. In providing surface protection, preliminary shore bombardment and gunfire support to amphibious operations, the **IOWAS** have brought back the pinpoint accuracy of the big gun which has been sorely lacking for so many years.

*With the ship at full dress and lined with bunting the crew mans the rail as the **IOWA** is recommissioned at Ingalls Shipbuilding, Pascagoula, MS on 28 April 1984. Vice President George Bush officiated at the ceremonies.*

The battleships compete for funding in the Navy's budget and critics of the program have been quick to point this out. Since the return of the battleships to the active Navy, it has been obvious that the advantages of their presence far outweigh the cost of the program. The cost to modernize and recommission a battleship seems to be less than the cost of a new frigate. While they are more expensive to operate than most surface ships, their capabilities are many times greater. For example, against a typical shore bombardment target, an **IOWA's** 16-inch guns can deliver conventional munitions, in tons per hour, at a rate of about two and a half times faster than a carrier. In a routine mission of this type, it would be unnecessary to commit valuable aircraft and their crews to provide fire power against coastal targets.

Another dimension that the battleship brings to surface warfare is survivability. This is not to imply that a battleship can not be sunk, but to sink one would be a very difficult task.

Their heavy armor, torpedo defense system and watertight subdivision would not be easily defeated by any conventional weapons, including newer missiles such as the Exocet. They are among the most survivable ships afloat today.

ARMAMENT

Main Battery — 16-inch Guns

The 16-inch/50 caliber MK 7 gun[4] fires two basic rounds; a 2,700 pound AP (armor piercing) and a 1,900 pound HC (high capacity) shore bombardment projectile. Nine of these weapons are mounted in three three-gun turrets.[5] (See Ballistic Data table for performance data)

The gun is a lightweight built-up type consisting of a liner, tube, jacket, hoops, locking rings, a liner locking ring, and a yoke ring. Assembly is accomplished by heating and expanding each piece before sliding it into position over the tube. When the components cool and shrink a tight single unit is formed. The liner is rifled with 96 grooves 0.15 inches deep with a uniform right hand twist of one turn in 25 calibers.

Each gun is mounted on an individual slide with its own elevation drive. The assembly includes a breach mechanism, firing lock, gas ejector, and yoke. The individual gun and slide assemblies, the two sight stations and the rangefinder's station are located in separate flameproofed compartments in each turret.

The turrets are virtually identical, each consisting of an armored gun-house with rotating structure and a fixed structure. The gun pit and machinery flat extend below the shelf plate of the gun house and the upper roller track is attached to the underside of the pit pan plate. A central column extends down to the turret foundation supporting the rotating handling, or shell decks. The fixed structure is a circular foundation bulkhead, or stool. The lower roller track is atop the stool and the rotating structure is supported by roller bearings between the roller tracks. The fixed handling, or shell decks are supported from the stool sides. Turrets I and III have two shell decks and Turret II, being a deck higher, has three. The turret structure is protected by a barbette of heavy armor. There is a weather seal between the barbette and the gun house but the gun house is not supported by, nor does it rotate on the barbette. Most of the projectiles are stored on the fixed (outer) and rotating (inner) shell decks. Powder handling rooms are at the base of each stool adjacent to the magazines.

---

4 During the early 1938 studies which led to the **IOWA** class, the General Board seriously considered using the 18-inch/47 caliber gun developed by the BuOrd during the 1920s. Although it did present some advantages, especially the penetration of plunging fire at extended ranges, the 16-inch/50 caliber was considered an all around better weapon. Also, the design would have had to grow considerably, and the new 45,000 ton weight limit was taken seriously in the **IOWA** design.

5 They are designated three-gun turrets, as opposed to triple turrets, because each gun is mounted on an individual slide with its own elevation drive. A triple turret has a single slide providing bearing surfaces for all three guns and uses a common elevation drive.

The IOWA is shown in drydock for overhaul at the Portsmouth Naval Shipyard, Portsmouth, VA in June 1985. The captain, executive officer and crew members proudly display the battle efficiency "E" recently awarded to the ship.

*On 31 July 1985 the **IOWA** left Portsmouth and proceeded to Whiskey Anchorage in Hampton Roads for loading gun ammunition. An ammunition barge and crane are alongside and 16-inch ammunition is being transferred to the fantail. At right: Projectiles waiting to be uncrated and struck down. In the foreground is a 2,700 pound MK 8 AP projectile with its rotating band exposed.*

Main Battery — Projectiles

The armor piercing round is the MK 8 projectile with a 1.5% bursting charge. It uses the MK 21 BDF (Base Detonating Fuze/.033 sec. delay) and requires a resistance equal to 1½ inches of armor for activation. Full, special and reduced charges can be used with the MK 8 projectile. The special and reduced charges, with their resultant lower muzzle velocity, give the projectile a steeper angle of fall with a trajectory similar to the 16-inch/45 caliber gun (See Ballistic Data). The effect of the steeper trajectory would be to shrink an armored surface target's immune zone at the outer end. It would also enhance defilade (reverse slope) capability against land targets.

The standard shore bombardment round is the MK 13 projectile with a 8.1% bursting charge. It can use either the MK 29 PDF (Point Detonating Fuze) or the MK 48 BDF (.015 sec. delay). There are two special MK 13 HC rounds using steel nose plugs. The first round uses a MK 55 ADF (Auxiliary Detonating Fuze) and a MK 48 BDF. The second uses a MK 21 BDF. Another round is the MK 13 HE (High Explosive) fuzed with a M564 MTF (Mechanically Timed Fuze/100 second capability).

Four new special purpose projectiles now in service use the MK 13 body. They are the MK 143 HE, which uses the Army M732 CVT (Controlled Variable Time) proximity fuze; the MK 144 ICM (Improved Conventional Munition) fuzed by the M724 ETF (Electronically Timed Fuze) which dispenses 400 M 43A1 wedge grenades; the MK 145 HE with the M724 ETF; and the MK 146 ICM using the M724 ETF to dispense 666 shaped charge bomblets.

A sub-caliber extended range projectile is being developed which is a 13-inch (approx.) spin stabilized round with a sabot adapting it to the 16-inch bore. The sabot is discarded after the round exits the muzzle. The flight weight of the projectile is 1,000 pounds and when fired with a full charge of powder has a muzzle velocity of over 3,600 ft./sec. It is capable of ranges in excess of 70,000 yards.

Main Battery — Propellant

Propelling charges for gun ammunition use smokeless powder, or SP, which is a uniform ether-alcohol colloid of purified nitrocellulose. A small quantity of diphenylamine or ethyl centralite is added for stability. Other additives are used to obtain suitable form, burning character and stability. (See Powder Chart in Ballistic Data)

Two types of 16-inch/50 caliber SP Propellants are in use. They are referred to as NALC/DODIC (Naval Ammunition Logistics Code/Department of Defense Inventory Code) code: D839 and D846. D839 is the original 16-inch/50 caliber powder and D846 is 16-inch/45 caliber powder. D839 propellant is authorized for use with the MK 8 and MK 13 type projectiles,

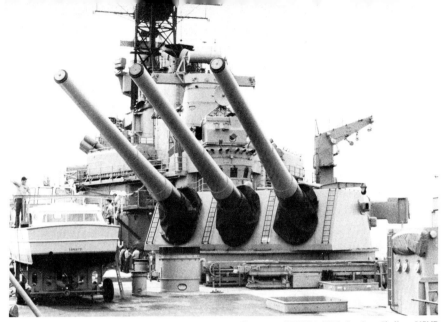

These three views of Turret III clearly show details of the massive structure. Above: an excellent view of the 16-inch/50 caliber MK 7 gun. Above right: The back of the turret showing the access hatch and ventilating system. Below right: The buckler has been removed from gun number 1 to repair blast damage. Note the extension tubes and clamping bands.

but D846 propellant is authorized for use with the MK 13 projectile only.

Even though the powder is stowed under special conditions, it deteriorates in time and this affects the muzzle velocity of the projectile producing erratic range and dispersion of the shot. In order to reduce the variation in muzzle velocity, the propellant is thoroughly remixed to evenly distribute the varying grains. Originally mixed in 600,000 pound lots, it is remixed in lots of 100,000 and rebagged to a tolerance of 1/10 of a pound per bag. It is then fired in two guns for charge weight assessment. The resulting round-to-round muzzle velocity variation is very low.

Gun life is expressed as the number of ESR (Equivalent Service Rounds) that can be fired before the gun must be relined. As designed, the life of the 16-inch/50 caliber MK 7 gun was determined to be 290 ESR, based on the 2,700 pound AP projectile fired with a full charge producing a muzzle velocity of 2,500 ft./sec. When firing a lighter projectile and/or using lighter charges, liner wear is considerably reduced.

Each time a gun is fired, the rotating band of the projectile erodes the liner as it travels the length of the bore. The development of wear reducing jackets of titanium dioxide and wax and polyurethane foam have greatly reduced liner erosion. Data on the titanium dioxide jacket indicates that wear may be reduced as much as 60%. No hard data is available yet on the polyurethane jacket but early indications are that it will be even more effective than the titanium dioxide jacket.

Courtesy of FCCM (SW) Stephen Skelley, USNR

Secondary Battery — 5-inch Guns

The double purpose 5-inch/38 caliber MK 12 gun fires two basic rounds: an AAC (antiaircraft common) and HC. The round is semifixed with a 54 pound projectile and 28 pound shell case, which includes a 15 pound powder charge. A limited number of special purpose illuminating and WP (smoke) projectiles are also carried. The AAC rounds use a VT (variable-timed) proximity fuze[6] to detonate the projectile when it comes close enough to the target to cause fragment damage.

As designed, the **IOWA's** secondary battery consisted of twenty 5-inch guns in ten twin mounts. Two mounts were located on each side of the 01 level and three were on each side of the 02 level. The large superstructure restricted their arcs of fire and they were most effective against targets approaching abeam. The crowded superstructure did not allow placing any 5-inch mounts on the centerline. During the 1982-1984 modernization the battery was reduced by eight guns. The two aftermost mounts on each side of the 02 level were removed to make room for the addition of missile batteries.

The gun is capable of a higher rate of fire than the gun crews can handle. An experienced crew can maintain a rate of 15 rounds per minute and as many as 22 rounds per minute at ideal loading angles. The IOWA carried a 5-inch practice loading machine on which the gun crews could drill to maintain their proficiency. During the 1982-1984 modernization the practice loader was removed and the gun crews drill on their actual weapons.

Courtesy of FCCM (SW) Stephen Skelley, USNR

The IOWA's secondary battery consists of twin 5-inch/38 caliber double purpose mounts. Above: The left side of Mount No. 52 with the guns at their maximum elevation of 85 degrees. Above right: The right side of Mount No. 53. The handling rooms, where ready service ammunition is stored, are directly below the base rings of the mounts. Two hoists service each handling room from the magazines, one for projectiles and one for powder.

6 The VT fuze carries a self-contained radio transmitter-receiver. When the projectile comes within effective range of the target an echo of the transmission is reflected back to the receiver causing detonation.

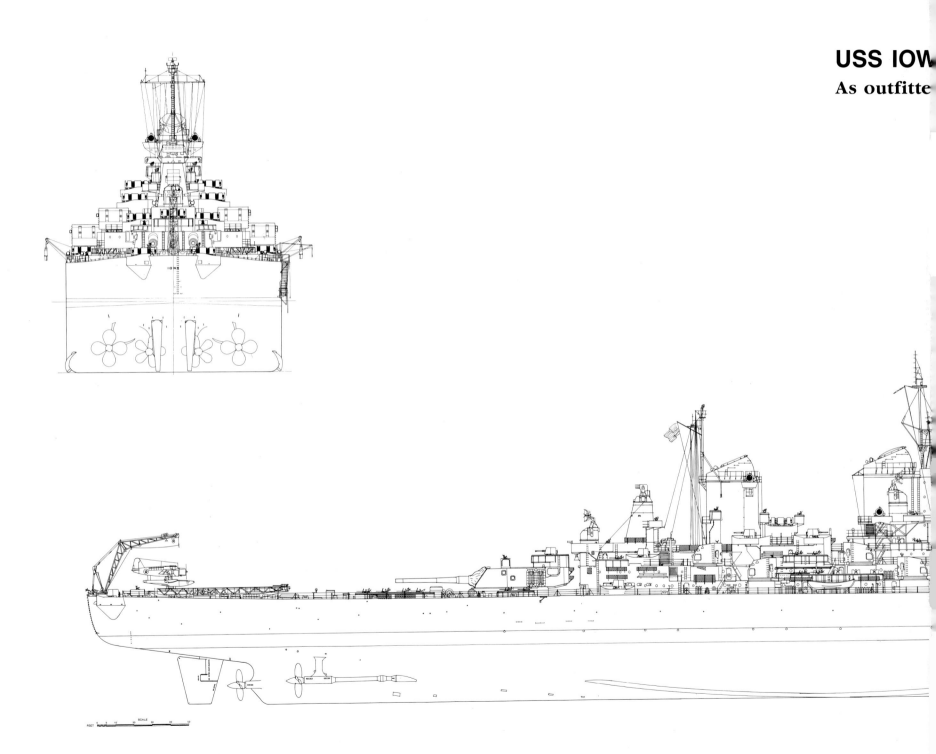

USS IOW

As outfitte

Drawn by Thomas F. Walkowiak

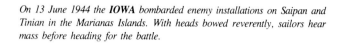

On 13 June 1944 the **IOWA** bombarded enemy installations on Saipan and Tinian in the Marianas Islands. With heads bowed reverently, sailors hear mass before heading for the battle.

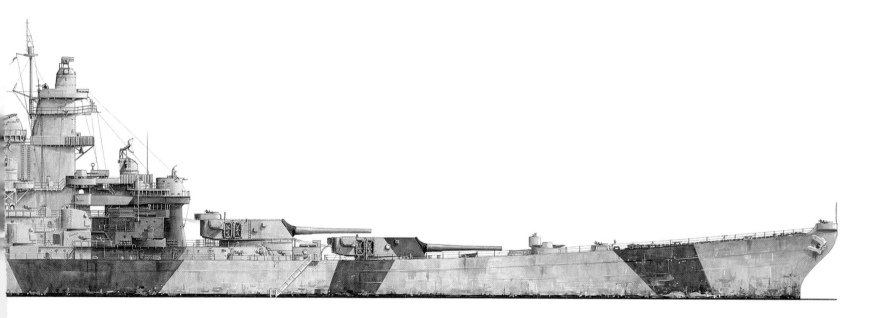

USS IOWA (BB 61)

As outfitted 1944

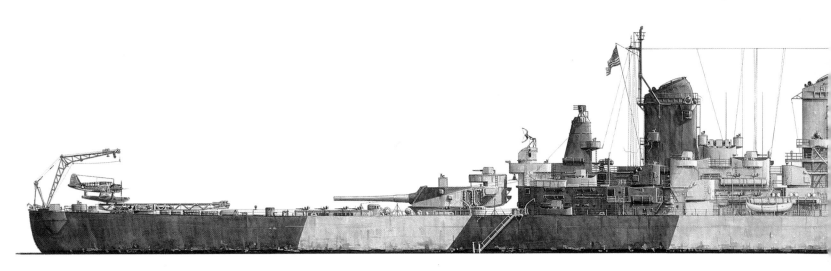

Rendering by Paul Bender

/A (BB 61)

d July 1942

BOW VIEW

61

"SALUTE TO LIBERTY"

by Tom Freeman

A MK 143 ABL raised to the firing position with four Tomahawk BGM-109 series cruise missiles. The Tomahawk gives the **IOWA** *a long range strike capability against surface and land targets. One of the land attack versions is configured for a nuclear warhead.*

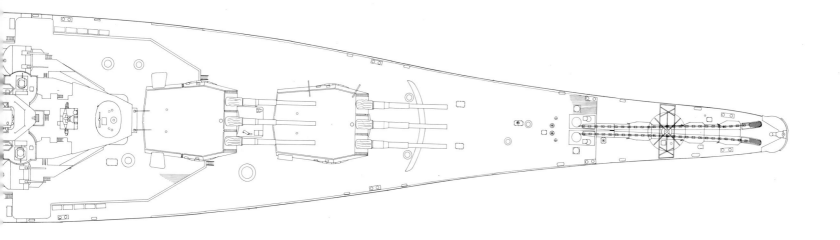

USS IOWA (BB 61)
As outfitted December 1986

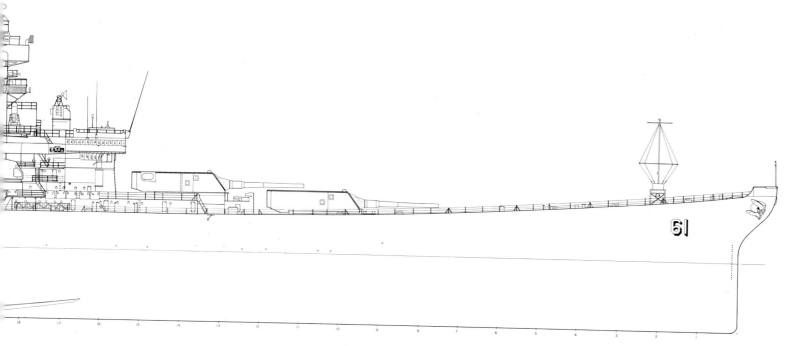

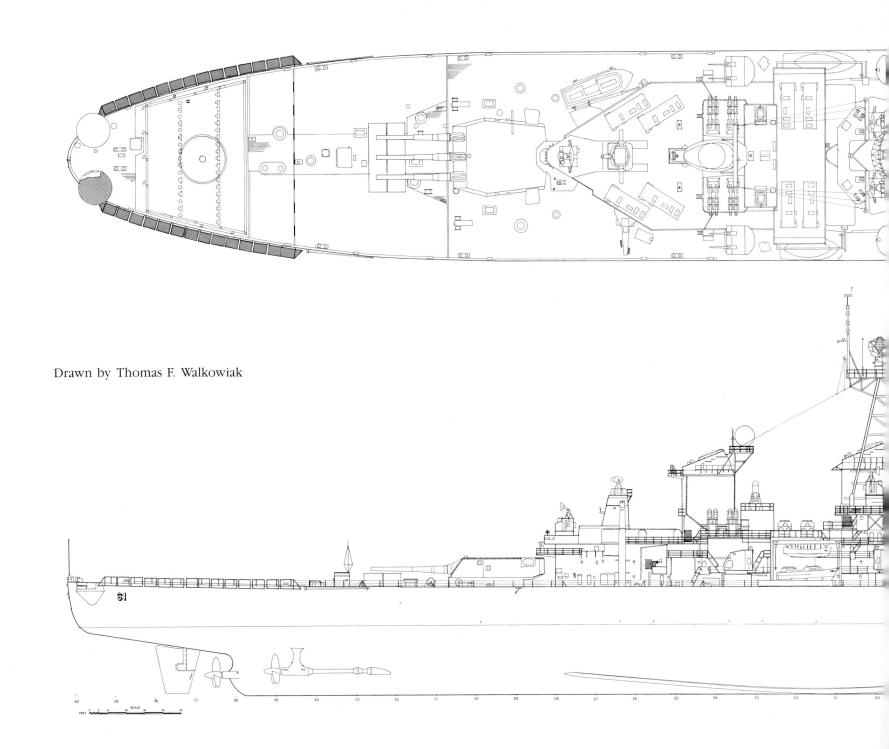

Drawn by Thomas F. Walkowiak

*The **IOWA** fires a salvo from Turrets I and II in August 1984 while operating off the Pacific Coast of Central America.*

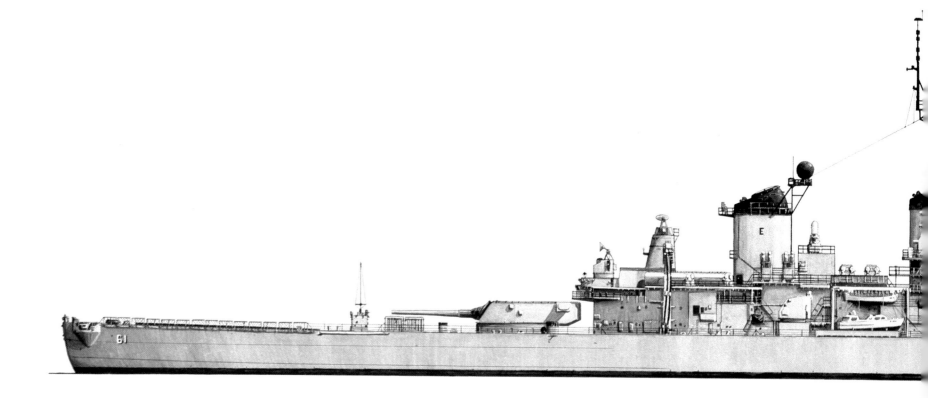

USS IOWA (BB 61)
As outfitted December 1986

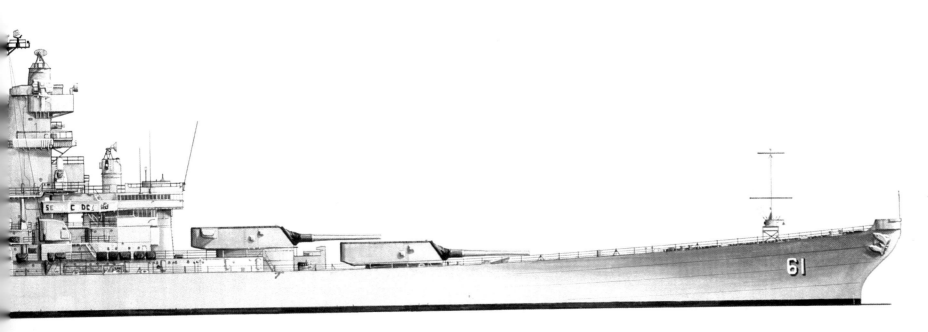

Rendering by Paul Bender

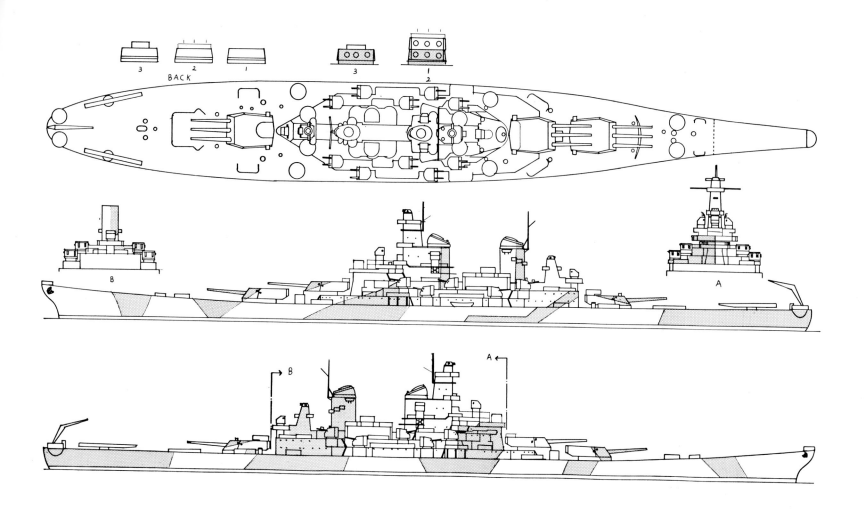

Camouflage Design — USS IOWA (BB 61)*

CAMOUFLAGE

This anti-submarine camouflage measure was developed in 1943. Photographic evidence suggests that this measure was applied in late December 1943 or in early January 1944. Colors on the vertical surfaces were Navy Blue 5-N and Light Gray 5-L. Decks and other horizontal surfaces were Deck Blue 20-B. As originally applied the vertical colors were blended by a sprayed feathered edge. The vertical colors were later brought together in sharp edges as shown above and by mid 1944 the port side area amidships was filled in with Navy Blue.

In January 1945, during an overhaul at Hunter's Point, the **IOWA** was painted in Measure 22 camouflage. According to this pattern, all vertical surfaces were painted Haze Gray 5-H with a Navy Blue band on the hull parallel to the waterline from the lowest point of sheer down. She finished the war in this pattern.

In 1946 the **IOWA** was painted in standard Haze Gray on all vertical surfaces and Deck Blue on all decks and horizontal surfaces. Large shaded hull numbers were also introduced on battleships during the post World War II period.

*No official reference was found for the measure or design numbers for this system. This system is Measure 32. It is believed that this is the first design in Measure 32 for a battleship or 1 B. The system has, therefore, been referred to as Measure 32: Design 1 B.

Antiaircraft Battery

The double purpose 5-inch/38 caliber guns can be used against aircraft as well as surface targets. The U.S. Navy had also developed new intermediate and close range weapons in an effort to literally throw up a blanket defense against enemy aircraft as they approached.

The 40 mm gun was the standard intermediate range weapon during World War II and the Korean War. An adaptation of the Swedish Bofors, it was originally developed in Germany by Krupp near the end of World War I. The standard for the **IOWAs** was a quadruple mount and the **IOWA** carried 19 for a total of 76 barrels. The mounts were distributed along the main deck and in the superstructure so as to obtain the greatest arcs of fire possible. Each gun was capable of firing a two pound shell at the rate of 160 rounds per minute. This was one of the more potent antiaircraft weapons of World War II.

The 20 mm gun was the standard close range weapon during World War II. Although considered obsolete by 1946 it was still carried by many ships during Korean War deployments. An adaptation of the Swiss Orlikon, it was a free-swinging mount requiring no external power source and could be literally bolted anywhere. The **IOWA** carried 52 of these mounts located in every area of the main deck from the very bow to the stern and they were spotted throughout almost every level of the superstructure. The gun could fire a shell slightly over a quarter of a pound at the rate of 450 rounds per minute.

*The **IOWA**'s original antiaircraft battery consisted of quadruple 40 mm and single 20 mm mounts. Above: A 40 mm MK 2 mount in an STS gun tub. Above right: Looking down on the same mount. In addition to the gun tub, the mount also has its own splinter shield. The slotted racks hold clips of four shells. Below right: Three 20 mm MK 4 mounts protected by an STS splinter shield. The boxes between the mounts contain ready service magazines.*

The new 20 mm MK 15 Phalanx CIWS is intended as a final defense against anti-ship missiles. The IOWA has four systems which provide a full 360 degree target coverage. When fully automatic, the system will engage any high speed incoming target. It has no IFF and will search, track, fire, kill assess and return to search.

The IOWA carries sixteen RGM-84 Harpoon missiles which give her an over-the-horizon strike capability against surface targets. Eight missiles are in these two quadruple MK 141 Kelvar armored canisters. The Harpoon has a range of up to 85 nm depending on the firing mode.

As the speed of aircraft increased, and suicide tactics such as the kamikazes became more commonplace, the 20 mm became less and less effective. Either a heavier shell was required or the density of fire needed to be increased. A heavier weapon would take time to develop so the BuOrd designed a twin version of the 20 mm in order to further saturate the anti-aircraft pattern. The Armament Summaries of the BuOrd indicate that the **IOWA** was fitted with eight twin 20 mm mounts in 1945 for evaluation purposes. From available photographs it is uncertain that this installation was ever carried out. Eventually the original 20 mm was removed from all of the **IOWA** class.

During the **IOWA's** 1982-1984 modernization, four new 20 mm MK 15 Phalanx CIWS (Close-In Weapons System) were installed. As a final defense against anti-ship missiles, the four systems provide full 360 degree target coverage. The weapon is a six-barrel Gatling gun capable of firing 3,000 rounds/minute (six barrels at 500 rounds/minute each). The MK 15 uses an adaptation of the M61 Vulcan gun used by the Air Force. It fires a MK 149 round which consists of a 12.75 mm sub-caliber penetrator, a sabot adapting the penetrator to the 20 mm bore, a pusher which imparts spin to the penetrator and a 20 mm shell casing. The sabot and pusher are discarded after the round exits the muzzle. The penetrator is a heavy metal bullet made of depleted uranium and its maximum effective range is 2,000 yards.

Missile Battery

The **IOWA** received a long range strike capability during her 1982-1984 modernization by the addition of the Harpoon and Tomahawk weapons systems. The Harpoon Weapon System is an anti-ship system and the Tomahawk Weapon System can be used against surface and land targets. The Tomahawk system also provides the **IOWA** with a nuclear capability.

The **IOWA** has two complete Harpoon systems which consist of four MK 141 launchers and sixteen RGM-84 missiles. Each MK 141 launcher holds a cluster of four Kelvar armored canisters in which the missiles are stored and from which they are fired at a fixed angle.

When fired, the booster propels the missile away from the ship approximately five miles and is discarded. The turbojet engine propels the missile from booster separation to the target. The stabilizing and actuator fins are stored folded in the canister and spring out into position after launching. During the flight the actuator fins receive inputs from the guidance system directing the missile to the target.

The **IOWA** has two complete Tomahawk systems which consist of thirty two BGM-109 series missiles in eight ABLs (Armored Box Launcher). Each MK 143 ABL holds a cluster of four AURs (All-Up-Round) consisting of a canister and the missile. The Tomahawk BGM-109 series has three basic configurations, the TASM (Tomahawk Anti-Ship Missile), TLAM-C (Tomahawk Land-Attack Missile - Conventional) and TLAM-N (Tomahawk Land-Attack Missile - Nuclear). The ABL is mounted horizontally with front end access to the canisters. The canister cluster is attached to the top of the ABL which is hydraulically raised to the firing position.

When fired, the booster propels the missile away from the ship approximately eleven miles and is discarded. The turbofan engine propels the missile from booster separation to the target. The wings and actuator fins are stored folded in the canister and spring out into position after launching. During the flight the actuator fins receive inputs from the guidance system directing the missile to the target.

Courtesy of FCCM (SW) Stephen Skelley, USNR

*The **IOWA** has a long range strike capability against surface and land targets with the BGM-109 series Tomahawk missiles. Thirty-two missiles are carried in eight MK 143 ABLs. The Tomahawk also has a nuclear capability against land targets. Above: The firing end of two ABLs. For firing, the top half of the ABL with its cluster of four missiles is elevated to a fixed firing angle. Below: The blast end of an ABL. The trunion for elevating the launcher can be seen in the lower corner of this end. The round doors are opened for blast exhaust when firing.*

Courtesy of FCCM (SW) Stephen Skelley, USNR

Turrets I and II are trained to starboard during gunnery exercises early in 1986. The MK 38 main battery director and its MK 13 radar, atop the fire control tower, are trained with the guns. These are two of the primary elements of the main battery fire control system.

FIRE CONTROL, RADAR, AND ELECTRONICS

Main Battery

The system to control the fire of the main battery is the MK 38 GFCS (Gun Fire Control System). Two systems are installed, consisting of the following primary elements:

- MK 38 directors/rangefinders/radar
- MK 40 director/optics/radar
- turret rangefinders
- spotting aircraft
- plotting rooms/system components

When the **IOWA** was designed radar was only in the developmental stage and fire control was effected through a system of optical rangefinders, telescopes, periscopes and spotting glasses in the main battery turrets and directors. The addition of radar greatly enhanced the system for it provided for target acquisition and spotting of shot at night, in fog, through smoke and all blind firing conditions.

The primary rangefinders were placed in the main battery turrets under the protection of their heavy armor. Long-base (46') rangefinders were incorporated in the after end of each turret. The rangefinder in Turret I was a coincidence type while those in Turrets II and III were stereoscopic.

The additional long-base (26.5') stereoscopic rangefinders were installed in the MK 38 directors and placed aloft atop the forward and after fire control towers. The height of these rangefinders (116' forward and 68' aft) provided initial ranges at a much greater distance than those in the turrets, however, they could not be nearly as well protected and, therefore, could be brought down more easily as the battle range closed. The fall of shot was spotted from the directors which provided corrections for the next salvo.

By the time the **IOWA** was completed, fire control radar had advanced considerably and two MK 8 units were installed, one atop each of the MK 38 directors. These units provided range and bearing information for surface targets and were capable of spotting shell splashes in both range and deflection. An improved unit, the MK 13, was later installed and is still in service today.

The MK 40 director was mounted in the roof of the armored conning tower. It consisted of two MK 30 and one MK 32 periscopes mechanically linked together. The MK 30s furnished director train and the MK 32 was used for spotting. The MK 9 spotting glass, normally a part of the MK 40 director was not installed on the **IOWA.**

During her post shakedown overhaul in July 1943, the **IOWA** received a MK 3 radar for ranging. This was intended as a functional substitution

The MK 38 director and its MK 13 radar are clearly detailed in these photos taken in January 1952 shortly after the **IOWA's** reactivation for Korean service. Just above the MK 13 is the SPS-6 air search radar and above that is an SG-6 surface search set. The array above the SG-6 is an AT-150 TBS. An interesting array of ECM gear is located on the yardarm. From the yard ends inboard are the "derby" and "sword" intercept antennas, anemometers and a "ski pole" BK-7 antenna to starboard only.

for the MK 9 spotting glass. A MK 27 radar replaced the MK 3 set in 1945 and it remained aboard until 1955.

Since the **IOWA** was recommissioned in 1984, DR-810 radar velocimeters have been installed on each of the main battery turrets. They are located on the turret roof over the center gun just behind the faceplate. The velocimeter tracks each round fired providing a quick and accurate assessment of muzzle velocity. This greatly improves the accuracy of subsequent fire.

The ship's aircraft were an important element of the fire control system. In addition to locating the enemy much in advance of when they could be seen from the fire control towers, they spotted the fall of shot and relayed target range information for the correction of following salvos. The aircraft complement of the **IOWA** was three float planes. Two catapults for launching the aircraft were located aft, one on each side of the fantail. There was no hangar to house the aircraft so they were stored either on the catapult in their launching cradle or on deck between the catapults. When commissioned the **IOWA** carried three OS2U Kingfishers which were later replaced by the newer SC-1 Seahawk. The U.S. Navy continued to use spotter aircraft after World War II and the **IOWA** carried two Seahawks as late as mid-1947. Her catapults were removed when she was reactivated for Korean service.

Late in 1986 the **IOWA** received the first aircraft she had carried since her Seahawks were landed in 1947. The aircraft is the Pioneer RPV

(Remotely-Piloted Vehicle) The **IOWA's** Pioneer RPV System consists of a ground control station, two portable control stations and eight RPVs. The system missions are reconnaissance, surveillance, search and rescue, weapons targeting and battle damage assessment. The first successful RPV flight and recovery on board the **IOWA** was 12 December 1986.

The plotting rooms are located deep within the armored citadel of the ship and house the remaining vital components of the MK 38 GFCS. One plotting room is located forward on the first platform and one is aft on the third deck. Each contains a MK 8 rangekeeper, a MK 41 stable vertical, a MK 48 bombardment computer and a fire control switchboard.

The MK 8 rangekeeper is a mechanical-analog computer into which target motion, ship's motion, ballistic and stabilization data are fed. The target's course and speed are plotted to predict its position when the shells will hit. From this information gun elevation and turret train orders are generated.

The MK 41 stable vertical is a gimbelled gyroscope that measures the roll and pitch of the ship in reference to the line of sight established by the director. This information is fed to the MK 8 rangekeeper for generating the gun orders.

The fire control switchboards control all of the inputs and outputs of the various components of the MK 38 GFCS. Through these switchboards either of the plotting rooms and the various elements of the fire control system can be selectively interchanged.

The MK 37 director controlled the fire of the 5-inch/38 caliber twin mounts against surface and air targets. The IOWA has four MK 37 systems. They are located as high as practical with one on the centerline forward, one starboard, one port, and one on the centerline aft giving full 360 degree target coverage. Above: The aft director is just above the landing control station. Below: The port director is trained outboard. The antenna is for the MK 25 radar.

Secondary Battery

The MK 37 director is designed to control the 5-inch/38 caliber double purpose guns against either air or surface targets, and to provide illumination control for star shells and searchlights. The MK 37 GFCS is a linear-rate system in many respects similar to the main battery system described above. It measures target position in three coordinates; range, relative target bearing, and target elevation. Three major units comprise a complete system; a director with radar, a stable element, and a computer with associated instruments at the gun. The **IOWA** has four MK 37 systems.

The directors are located fairly high in the superstructure to give the best target coverage possible. One is located on top of the pilot house overlooking the conning tower, one is atop the end of the after superstructure, and one is located on each side of the forward stack at the approximate level of the forward unit. The computers and stable elements are located in the plotting rooms which are adjacent to the main battery plotting rooms.

The director is equipped with a stereoscopic rangefinder (15' base), two telescopes, and a slewing sight. The control officer can rapidly designate a target and bring it into the field of the optics with the slewing sight. The **IOWA** carried a MK 4 radar antenna atop each director house when completed. These were replaced with MK 12/22 units during her 1945 refit. The antennas and director optics were aligned. Either one could be used alone, or they could be used in combination, thus providing optimum tracking accuracy. The MK 12/22 antenna was replaced during the **IOWA's** 1955 overhaul with the newer, more accurate, MK 25 antenna.

In the plotting rooms, the stable element establishes a horizontal reference plane through use of a gyroscope, so that level and crosslevel can be measured. This information is fed to the adjacent computer which makes the calculations required for control of the double purpose battery. The resultant is in turn relayed to the director to maintain the line of sight to the target and as gun orders to the turrets for aiming the guns.

Antiaircraft Battery

The simple lightweight MK 51 director was developed for control of the 40mm power driven gun mount. The MK 51 is a relative-rate system incorporating the MK 14 gunsight. Directors were located near the gun mounts they controlled, usually just above the mount to be relatively free from its vibration and smoke. Ring sights and handcranks were also mounted on the 40mm gun mounts for manually pointing, training, and firing the guns.

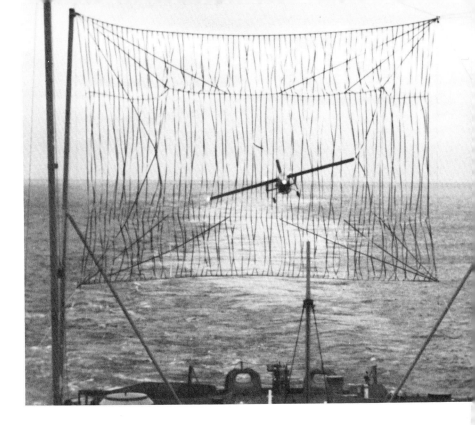

*Late in 1986 the **IOWA** received a Pioneer RPV system and an air group designated VC-6. Eight Pioneer vehicles are carried in blast proof hangars just aft of Turret III. The system is used for target acquisition, surveillance, gunfire spotting and damage assessment. Above: A Pioneer is launched during a rocket-booster assisted takeoff from the flight deck of the **IOWA** in December 1986. Note the recovery net erected on the stern. Right: After a successful flight, the Pioneer approaches the recovery net on the stern. The system can operate out to a range of 110 miles and has an endurance of eight hours.*

During her 1955 refit the **IOWA** had six MK 56 GFCS installed. These were intended for her 3-inch/50 caliber battery which was not installed (See Armament Summary). The MK 56 was a dual-ballistic system capable of issuing simultaneous gun orders to two different sized batteries. It was used to control the 40mm guns and gave them a blind firing capability. It could also be used to control the 5-inch/38 battery.

The 20mm free-swinging gun mount was equipped with a ring sight for aiming, and pointing and training was effected by the operator's body movement through a set of handle bars and shoulder rests. It was necessary for the operator to lead the target in both traverse and elevation. Usually, every fifth round in the belt was a tracer which assisted the operator in spotting his fire. The MK 14 gun sight was designed to control antiaircraft machine guns against rapidly moving targets at short ranges using a lead angle computing mechanism. The sight could be mounted on either the single or twin 20mm mounts, and as mentioned above was the primary element of the MK 51 director.

The 20mm MK 15 Phalanx CIWS is controlled by the AN/VPS-2 pulsed doppler type search and track radar. It tracks the target and the outgoing rounds and corrects for the angular difference between them. When in fully automatic the system will search, track, fire, kill assess and return to search. The system has no IFF (Identification Friend or Foe) and any high speed incoming target will be engaged.

Missile Battery

The RGM-84 Harpoon and BGM-109, T-ASM Tomahawk weapons control systems are similar, both using active radar for homing in. The T-LAM Tomahawk uses inertial guidance and is targeted by TERCOM (Terrain Contour Matching).

The IOWA enters a floating drydock at an advanced base in December 1944. Her radar, fire control and electronics suit is an interesting mixture of, probably, field installations and modifications. Her air search radar is the large SK "bedspring" at the foretop and the SG surface search sets are on the platform on the control tower and the maintop. Elements of the MK III IFF system are visible with the small BL "bedspring" atop the SK and the BK-7 "ski poles" on the fore and after yards. The ECM gear is unusual. An AS-56 antenna is on the starboard fore yard and AS-37 "wagon wheels" can be seen on the forward and after ends of the air defense level. Two TDY jammers are clearly visible, one on each side of the control tower, and a DBM antenna appears to be on the starboard side of the air defense level opposite the AS-37 antenna. The main battery fire control radar is the MK 8 and the secondary battery radar is the MK 4.

Search Radar

When the **IOWA** was completed her radar suit consisted of the new SK and two SG sets. The SK was mounted on a round platform atop the stub foremast just above the MK 8 fire control antenna on Spot 1. The first production models of the SK became available in January 1943 and the **IOWA** was one of the early installations. One SG set was placed on a platform on the forward end of the fire control tower just below the air defense station and the second unit was installed atop the pole mainmast.

Long range aircraft detection was provided by the SK air search set. Its 17' square antenna had a range of 100 nm and a height capability of 10,000' at that range.

Ship detection was furnished by the two SG surface search sets. A small waveguide fed unit, SG could detect large ships at over 20 nm and aircraft under 500' at about 15 nm. Its displays of vessels, as well as land masses, made it useful to navigation.

In early 1945 the **IOWA** was refitted at Hunter's Point. During this period she received a new foremast with a foretop and foretopmast. The SK antenna and a new SU surface search set were installed on the foretop. The SK was forward and the SU aft of the topmast. The SU had a small dish antenna enclosed in a radome. A similar, but smaller, maintopmast was fitted to the mainmast and the light tripod supported by the stack received heavier legs. The after SG set was relocated to the maintopmast and a new SR air search set was mounted on the maintop. The foreward SG set was removed and replaced with a TDY jamming unit and a DBA radio direction-finder was mounted on the foretopmast.

In October 1946, during a brief availability at the Puget Sound Naval Shipyard, the **IOWA's** SK was replaced with the SK-2. This later model had a 17' dish antenna which somewhat reduced the side lobe pattern but by this time both SK models were considered obsolescent.

In her 1948 refit the **IOWA** received an SP air intercept radar replacing the SR set. To mount the SP a new tripod mainmast was fitted on the after stack replacing the pole and the new antenna was installed on the maintop. During this availability period she also received an SG-6, replacing the DBA on her foretopmast and the aft SG was placed on a new maintopmast. The **IOWA** was deactivated in 1949 and placed in reserve with this radar configuration.

When the **IOWA** was reactivated for Korean service at Long Beach in 1951 she landed her SK-2 air search set for the SPS-6 with a horn-fed 18' x 5' parabolic antenna.

The last change to the **IOWA's** radar suit before she was again placed in the Reserve Fleet was in 1955 at the Norfolk Naval Shipyard. Two new radars were installed, an SPS-12 air search set and an SPS-8 air search/height finding set. The SPS-12 was a heavier and improved SPS-6 requiring only

The **IOWA** is shown at anchor in San Francisco Bay off the Naval Air Station in Alameda on 22 May 1947. Her air search radars are the SK-2 on the foretop and an SR set on the maintop. There is an SU surface search set in the dome on the aft end of the foretop and an SG set on the maintopmast. The ECM gear visible includes a DBA radio direction-finder on the foretopmast, an AS-56 antenna is on the futtock brace of the foremast and a TDY jammer is on the platform just below the air defense level.

The crew mans the rail as the **IOWA** leaves Pearl Harbor and passes Diamond Head on 28 October 1952 enroute to the East Coast and Norfolk for overhaul. Her new air search radars are an SPS-6 on the foretop and an SP air intercept on the maintop. Surface search sets include a new SG-6 on the foretopmast and the SG on the maintopmast. ECM gear visible is the TDY jammer below the air defense level and the DBM antennas have been relocated to a stub mast on the after stack.

AS-390/SRC
AT-150/SRC
AN/SPS-8

MK13/0
MK35/2

NORFOLK NAVAL SHIPYARD
PORTSMOUTH, VIRGINIA
USS IOWA BB61
ANTENNA SYSTEM

AS-390/SRC
AT-150/SRC
66095
SG-6
66095
66095
AN/SPS-12
AS-466/SR
MK13-0
66131
66046
66047
AS-177/U
AS-466/SR
66046
2
MK25/3
MK35/2
TDY-1A
MK25

NORFOLK NAVAL SHIPYARD
PORTSMOUTH, VIRGINIA

These photos taken on 18 February 1956 at the Norfolk Naval Shipyard show the IOWA's complete radar and electronics suit. This is probably the way she was decommissioned. Note the MK 56 directors for the 40 mm batteries. The MK 56 with the MK 35 radar gave the 40 mm a blind firing capability. The MK 56 was a dual-ballistic system which could also control the 5-inch guns and the 5-inch and 40 mm guns simultaneously.

minor modifications to the foremast. The SPS-8, however, was much heavier than its predecessor and required a new mainmast arrangement. A quadrapod mast was fitted with its after main legs extending down to the mainbrace for the kingpost tops and its forward legs were supported by the after stack. (During this overhaul, kingposts with 65' booms were fitted on the 02 level to handle the large boats nested on the main deck abeam the after main battery fire control director). The SPS-8 was installed on a new maintop. A new maintopmast was also fitted but the SG set was not put back.

When modernized in 1984 the **IOWA** received the latest in search radar; SPS 10 and SPS 49. A heavy new tripod foremast was fitted to accommodate these antennas and other electronic gear. The SPS 10 is an older but reliable surface search set which can effectively range to the horizon. The SPS 49 is the most effective air search set in use today by the U.S. Navy.

It has features for use with ECCM (Electronic Counter-Countermeasures) and ADT (Automatic Detection and Tracking).

Electronics

The **IOWA** was outfitted with a MK III IFF System when completed. The system was capable of identifying radar contacts and could furnish its identity to challenging signals with its interrogator and transponder units.

The BL interrogator sent out a coded signal. If the signal was received by a friendly contact it activated a transponder unit in the contact which sent out a favorable return signal. The antenna for the BL was mounted on the SK antenna frame. Both signals were sent out and received together but were displayed separately. The BL antenna is the small rectangular bedspring on top of the SK unit.

Some of the current radar and electronics equipment aboard the IOWA is shown in these two photos. Left: On the new foretop are the search radars SPS-10 (small) and SPS-49 (large). A portion of the MK II AIMS IFF system is on the foretopmast. Shown below the MK 13 fire control antenna is the SLQ-32 ECM antenna. Four SRBOK launchers can be seen around the base of the MK 37 director in canvas covers. The SLQ-32 and SRBOK are used in conjunction as a threat warning and countermeasures system. On the forward end of the air defense level is an OE-8 satellite communications antenna. Right: The radar antenna for controlling the RPVs is located on the forward side of the after stack. On the after side of the stack is another OE-8 antenna.

The BK transponder unit was activated by a signal from an interrogator and returned a favorable signal, as indicated previously. An unfriendly unit would be unable to respond with the proper signal and/or on the required frequency. The BK antenna resembled a "ski pole" and was placed as high as possible to avoid obstructions. The **IOWA** had three BK-7 antennas, two on the foreyard and one on the afteryard.

Currently the **IOWA** has a MK XII AIMS IFF system.

Electronic Counter Measures

From photographs taken in late 1945 it appears that the **IOWA** was fitted with two ECM (electronic counter measure) systems, a direct noise amplifier and a jammer.

Elements of a direct noise amplifier system are visible in the form of two AS-56 type dipole antennas, one on each side of the foremast back-

stay, and two AS-37 "wagon wheel" and dipole antennas, one on each side of the TDY platform. The noise was a continuous output and appeared as "grass" on the enemy's display.

A standard TDY jamming unit can be seen on a platform on the forward end of the fire control tower just below the air defense station. It appears that a DBM antenna is located on the port yard. Jamming was produced by the TDY unit in conjunction with the DBM antenna. The DBM furnished signal information to the incoming pulse, thus jamming the returning signal rendering it illegible.

When modernized the **IOWA** received the latest ECM gear including the SLQ 32(V)3 and eight MK 137 SRBOC (Super Rapid Blooming Offboard Chaff) launchers. The quick-reaction mode of the SLQ 32 can initiate jamming and launch SRBOC decoys against quickly appearing targets. Also installed was the SLQ 25 Nixie, a towed device designed to replace the ship as the target for a torpedo.

The *IOWA* is shown underway here in January 1944. This aerial broadside clearly shows the large area which had to be protected. The armored citadel of the vessel ranged from just forward of Turret No. I to just aft of Turret No. III. The viewing angle is near that of an approaching shell, close to the far side of the immune zone, which might penetrate some of the deck armor. Because of the inclination of the side armor, a shell approaching at this angle would probably glance off of the main belt.

PROTECTION

Armor Protection

Protection against gunfire was provided by heavy armor. Contrary to popular belief, protection was not specified in armor thickness, but rather by an immune zone. The immune zone can be expressed as having an inner and outer edge; the inner edge being the shortest range at which the side and deck armor can not be penetrated, and the outer edge being the shortest range at which plunging fire will penetrate the deck armor. In theory immunity is desired against a specific weapon, usually the main armament of the vessel itself, for it would overpower a weaker adversary and avoid contact with a more powerful one. The size of the zone would be determined by the expected battle ranges.

The **IOWA** class was designed to resist a 2,240 pound 16-inch/45 caliber shell between 18,000 and 30,000 yards. In June 1939, a year after the **IOWA** design had been fixed, a new 2,700 pound shell was adopted. The new and more powerful shell caused the immune zone to shrink to between 20,200 and 25,500 yards. Progress on the first two ships had advanced to the point where armor had already been ordered and there was no hope of any extensive revision to the armor protection system. Some minor improvements, however, were possible in BB 63 and subsequent ships of the class.

The armor protection of a battleship can be visualized as an armored box, or citadel, into which all of the vital equipment, such as machinery, magazines, plotting rooms, etc. necessary for survival, is fitted. Its usual length is from the forward end of the barbette for the first turret to the after end of the barbette for the last turret. Items outside the box requiring armor protection, such as turrets, conning tower, fire control directors, and steering gear, are connected to the box forming a sort of appendage.

The design of the armor protection system was essentially the same as for the **SOUTH DAKOTA** class. The side, or belt armor was inclined to 19 degrees and hung on the outboard side of No. 3 torpedo bulkhead from frame 50 forward of No. 1 barbette to frame 166 aft of No. 3 barbette. The main portion of the belt was 12.2 inches thick, extending from a lip just above the second deck to a lip just below the third deck. The secondary portion of the belt extended down from the lower lip to the inner bottom and was tapered from 12.2 inches to 1.4 inches. The 12.2 inches of armor sloped at 19 degrees was considered equivalent to 13.5 inches of vertical armor. Extending the armor down to the inner bottom was intended to protect against shells falling short and continuing under water. A portion of the main belt was continued aft to protect the steering gear leads.

The ends of the box were closed by armored transverse bulkheads. As originally designed these bulkheads were 11.3 inches thick and the **IOWA** and **NEW JERSEY** were so completed. When BB 63 and subsequent ships of the class were ordered, the weight restrictions of the Treaty were no longer in effect and these bulkheads were increased to 14.5 inches for added protection at a wider range of target angles.

The top of the box was covered with a system of armored decks which included protection against aerial bombs. The main deck was designated the bomb deck, the second deck was the main armor deck, and the splinter deck was a flat fitted just below the second deck only for the length of the box. The bomb deck was 1.5 inch STS, the main armor deck was 4.75 inch Class B armor laid on 1.25 inch STS, and the splinter deck was .625 inch STS. Within the immune zone the main armor deck was designed to defeat plunging shells which entered the side above the top of the main belt. The splinter deck was intended to catch any spall and pieces of armor which might be broken off. If the angle of fall was steep enough there would be the added protection of the armor on the bomb deck. The bomb deck was designed to detonate general purpose bombs on contact and arm armor piercing bombs so they would explode between the bomb deck and the main armor deck.

New ballistic plating was added to several spaces when the **IOWA** was modernized in 1982-1984. The spaces are located in the superstructure and include the new CEC (Combat Engagement Center) and Tomahawk, Harpoon and CIWS support spaces.

For details and thickness of armor for the conning tower, turrets, etc. see the General Data Table.

Underwater Protection

Protection against the effects of torpedoes, mining, and near miss bombing was provided by the side protective and triple bottom systems. Both systems were multi-layered and intended to absorb the energy from an underwater explosion equivalent to a 700-pound charge of TNT. This loading was determined as the result of an intelligence survey from the mid 1930s and when the **IOWA** class was designed, the U.S. Navy was unaware of the advances the Japanese had made in torpedo technology. One of the early unpleasant surprises of the Pacific War was the Japanese 24-inch "long lance" torpedo carried by most of their surface craft. They were also able to pack a considerably larger explosive charge, by U.S. standards, into their aerial and submarine torpedoes.

This aerial view of the IOWA taken 10 June 1944 gives a clear indication of the massive deck area which had to be protected against plunging shell fire and bombing. Relating this photograph to the one on the opposite page can help to understand the principle of an immune zone and the effect of oblique and plunging gun fire. Imagine a shell approaching near the inner end of the zone. It would have a rather flat trajectory and glance off of the deck, but would confront the side armor at about 20 degrees. Now imagine a shell approaching near the outer end of the zone. It would have a rather steep trajectory and would glance off of the side armor, but would confront the deck armor at a more favorable angle for penetration.

The side protection system consisted of four tanks on the outboard side of the hull extending from the third deck to the turn of the bilge. The tanks were inclined 19 degrees, the same as the armor belt which was attached to the third torpedo bulkhead inboard. The full tank system ranged from frame 50 forward of No. 1 barbette to frame 166 aft of No. 3 barbette. The two outboard tanks were liquid loaded with fuel oil or ballast and the two inboard tanks were kept void. In theory, the liquid layers would absorb the shock from an explosion and contain most of the shards from the

The two large stacks are the only external indication of the IOWA's massive main propulsion plant. Eight boilers furnish high pressure, superheated steam to four sets of geared steam turbines which drive four shafts. The plant produces 212,000 shaft horsepower which can drive the ship at over 33 knots. Each stack intakes air and exhausts flue gasses for four boilers. This view was taken in January 1944.

ENGINEERING

Propulsion

The propulsion plant can produce 212,000 horsepower which is necessary to meet the 33 knot speed requirement. Steam for the plant is furnished by eight boilers and delivered to four sets of geared turbines which are direct coupled to double reduction gears which drive the shafts. The propulsion machinery is distributed in an alternating fire room engine room arrangement with the main steam system fully cross-connected to each engine room.

The boilers are three drum double furnace express type, generating steam at 565 psi and 850 degrees F. The turbine group consists of one high pressure turbine, one low pressure turbine, and one double reduction gear. The high pressure turbine is coupled to the high speed high pressure pinion and the low pressure turbine is coupled to the high speed low pressure pinion of the reduction gear. The low pressure turbine contains an astern element in each end which can reverse the shaft rotation for backing down. The reduction gear reduces the high speed input from the turbines in two stages furnishing 202 rpm to the shafts to make 33 knots. All ancillary machinery for the main plant is located in the same space as the equipment it serves.

One of the improvements to the main propulsion plant during the **IOWA's** 1982-1984 modernization was the conversion of the boilers to burn standard Navy distillate fuel. The fuel oil storage and transfer system was also overhauled to handle the new fuel.

Auxiliaries

The electrical plant includes 8, 1,250 kw steam turbo-generators which furnish power to the hundreds of electrical motors that operate the ordnance, fire control, radar, and electronics equipment as well as the ship's hotel load. There are also 2, 250 kw emergency diesel generators which can furnish power if any or all of the ship's service generators fail.

Two turbo-generators are located in each machinery room adjacent to the main engines and steam supply. The emergency diesel generators are located in auxiliary machinery rooms, one forward and one aft of the main propulsion rooms. The forward auxiliary machinery room also contains the distilling plant. The large triple effect evaporators process sea water into feed water for the boilers and potable water for drinking, cooking, and personal cleaning.

An important support system installed during modernization was the sewage CHT (Collection, Holding and Transfer) system. The CHT system prevents the discharge of sewage into rivers, harbors and coastal waters.

For details and data for the engineering plant see General Data Table.

damaged structure. The first void was expected to contain any leakage and the belt, on its inboard side, was intended to stop any fragments which penetrated the second torpedo bulkhead. Hopefully this system would keep the second void and fourth torpedo or holding bulkhead intact protecting the machinery spaces. The system was shallowest at No. 1 and No. 3 barbettes, a consequence of the fineness of the hull form, but this defect had to be accepted for any increase in hull volume, especially around the forward barbette, would have resulted in a reduction of speed.

The triple bottom system consisted of two layers of tanks on the very bottom of the hull between the holding bulkheads of the side protection system. The tanks were formed by the shell at the bottom of the hull and the inner bottom and third bottom flats. The inner bottom ran the entire length of the ship but the third bottom was spread essentially under the vitals of the ship from frame 36 well forward of No. 1 barbette to frame 173 well aft of No. 3 barbette. The double bottom tanks were liquid loaded with fuel oil and reserve feed and potable water except near the ends where they were kept void. The third bottom tanks were all kept void. In theory the system was intended to absorb the shock of an underwater explosion and to function similarly to the side protection system.

HISTORY

The **USS IOWA (BB 61)** was launched 27 August 1942 at the New York Navy Yard. The fourth ship to bear the name of the 29th state, the **IOWA** is the namesake of her class. She and her sister ships represent the most powerful high-speed battleships built by the U.S. Navy. Weighing 45,000 tons and capable of a speed of over 30 knots, the **IOWA** was commissioned 22 February 1943. At her commissioning, then Secretary of the Navy Frank Knox declared the **IOWA** to be "the greatest ship ever launched by the American Nation."

Her first war assignment took her into the North Atlantic in August 1943 to neutralize the threat of the German battleship **TIRPITZ** in the waters off Norway. By fall of that year, she was on her way to Casablanca, North Africa, carrying President Franklin D. Roosevelt to the Teheran Conference due to take place in November 1943. A large, square bathtub installed for the use of the President remains today in the Captain's inport cabin as a reminder of that momentous trip. At the end of the Conference she returned the President to the United States and prepared to head for the Pacific war zone.

As flagship of Battleship Division Seven, the **IOWA** entered her first Pacific campaign on 23 January 1944 in support of carrier air strikes against the Kwajalein and Eniwetok Atolls, and then moved on to support the air attack against the Japanese naval base at Truk, in the Caroline Islands. On 16 February, she joined the **NEW JERSEY,** two cruisers, and four destroyers to sweep the seas around Truk and destroy escaping enemy vessels. As February drew to a close, she rejoined Vice Admiral Marc A. Mitscher's Fast Carrier Task Force 58 northeast of Truk and moved in to support the bombing strikes on Saipan, Tinian, Rota and Guam in the Marianas.

Again, in company with the **NEW JERSEY,** a carrier and destroyers, the **IOWA** participated in the bombardment of Mili Atoll in the Marshall Islands on 18 March. During the attack, the **IOWA** received her first hit when she was struck by two Japanese 4.7 projectiles. One burst on the deck and the other pierced her side and burst in an empty compartment, but neither caused significant damage.

On 30 March, the **IOWA** spent several days in support of air strikes against Palau and Woleai Islands in the Carolines and then steamed with Task Group 58 for New Guinea and air strikes on Hollandia, Aitape and Wake Islands. On 22 April 1944 she was among those ships supporting the Army landing at Aitape and Tanahmerah and Humboldt Bays. Before leaving the Caroline Islands, the **IOWA** took part in the bombardment of the bombs wharf, seaplane base and other enemy facilities on Ponape Island.

During the first half of June, as a unit of Vice Admiral Mitscher's Fast Carrier Task Force, the **IOWA** took part in the support of air strikes and the bombardment of enemy installations on Saipan, Tinian and other is-

The USS IOWA (BB 61) is launched at the New York Navy Yard on 27 August 1942. The ship was sponsored by Mrs. Henry A. Wallace, wife of the Vice President who is holding the christening bottle. The Wallaces were residents of Iowa.

lands of the Marianas. The month ended with the Task Force preparing for a major Japanese counter-offensive and the arrival of reinforcements led by Admiral Raymond A. Spruance.

The **IOWA** was on the battle line as the Japanese began the opening attack of the Battle of the Philippine Sea on 19 June 1944. In four massive raids, the Japanese launched 373 of their land and carrier based planes against the American force in what would come to be called "The Marianas Turkey Shoot." Only 130 of the enemy's carrier based planes returned to their ships. About 50 of their planes based on Guam were lost. Of the three hundred American carrier planes that took part in the battle, only 23 were shot down. Not a single ship of the Task Force was lost, and the **SOUTH DAKOTA** was the only one to receive a direct hit.

In the meantime, the Japanese fleet had suffered the loss of the carriers **TAIHO** and **SHOKAKU** to American submarines. On 20 June, Vice Admiral Mitscher launched long range air strikes against the remainder of the Imperial Fleet, causing the loss of the carrier **HIYO,** two tankers and damage to two other aircraft carriers and a battleship. The defeated Japanese fleet headed for Okinawa with just 35 aircraft still operational out of the 430 with which it began the Battle of the Philippine Sea.

The **IOWA** is shown here underway in the Pacific during 1944. She is in company with the **INDIANA** (BB 58). Note how her hull lines fine down forward.

Shown here in the summer of 1951, the **IOWA** is being reactivated for Korean War service. The gun bucklers have been removed to clean and service the gun ports. The bucklers, extension tubes and clamping bands can be seen on the turret roofs.

The **IOWA** continued in support of air strikes against bases in the Marianas and Carolines and then in September as a unit of Fleet Admiral William F. Halsey's Third Fleet participated in support of carrier strikes against the Philippines and the Carolines.

In October 1944, the **IOWA** became the press ship for the Fleet, providing facilities for leading newsmen to transmit their first-hand reports of the war. By 10 October, the **IOWA** was off Okinawa participating in air strikes against the Ryukyu Islands, Taiwan and Luzon which continued until 23 October and the Battle for Leyte Gulf.

During the battle, the **IOWA's** task group sank the Japanese 2,400 ton destroyer **NOWAKI.** Afterwards, she remained in Philippine waters supporting strikes against Luzon and Taiwan until December. At that time, the **IOWA** left the war zone for the United States and an overhaul at Hunters Point Shipyard in San Francisco which lasted from 15 January to 19 March 1945.

Shortly thereafter, the **IOWA** sailed for the Far East, via Pearl Harbor and Eniwetok, arriving off Okinawa in April 1945 to rejoin her former carrier task group and support operations in the air coverage of Okinawa. On 25 May, she supported air strikes against Kyushu, one of Japan's home islands, and then in July against Tokyo, and other targets on Honshu and Hokkaido. In shore bombardments, the **IOWA's** guns contributed to the destruction of steel mills and other facilities on Honshu and she continued in support of strikes against the Japanese homeland until the close of hostilities on 15 August 1945.

On 29 August 1945, the **IOWA** steamed into Tokyo Bay as one of the ships supporting the landing of occupation forces the next day. Her job in the Far East done, the **IOWA** left for the United States on 20 September. She arrived in Seattle, Washington on 15 October 1945 and went on to Long Beach, where until January 1946, she was engaged in training operations along the West Coast.

From 27 January 1946, when she arrived again in Tokyo Bay, until 25 March when she returned to Long Beach, the **IOWA** served as flagship of the Fifth Fleet. In the United States, she operated along the West Coast conducting drills, maneuvers and naval reserve and midshipmen training

*With the mountainous coast of North Korea in the background, the **IOWA** maneuvers into position for bombarding shore installations April 1952. This was her first action since World War II.*

*Shown here at Sasebo, Japan in June 1952, the **IOWA** loads ammunition and supplies. Sailors stand on 16-inch powder cans while handling 5-inch powder cans. After replenishment, the ship returned to the gun line along the east coast of Korea.*

cruises. Her inactivation began at San Francisco in September 1948 and she was placed out of commission in reserve on 24 March 1949.

The **IOWA's** inactivation was short-lived. With the escalating level of hostilities in Korea, the battleship was recommissioned 25 August 1951. Following gunnery exercises and training operations, she sailed for the Far East on 1 April 1952, and became the flagship of Vice Admiral Robert T. Briscoe, Commander of the 7th Fleet operating in support of the United Nations Forces in Korea.

Accompanied by the destroyer **MACKENZIE,** the **IOWA** conducted gun strikes against enemy supply routes in the Wonson-Songjin area on 8 April. The following day, she joined the bombline striking enemy troop concentrations, supply areas, and suspected gun positions in and around Suwon Dan and Kojo. She left the bombline for Wonsan Harbor on 14 April, there to bombard and destroy warehouses, observation posts and railroad marshalling yards. The **IOWA** then returned to the bombline in support of United Nations ground forces in the Konsong area.

After replenishment in Sasebo, Japan, she bombarded enemy supply routes in the vicinity of Mayang-do and Tachen and then went on to Teojo-

Sinpo where she came under fire from shore batteries on Mayang-do Island. With the aid of strikes from Task Force aircraft, the **IOWA** quickly silenced the guns on Mayang-do and went on to bombard other targets in the vicinity.

On 25 April, the **IOWA** struck north against Chongjin, the most important industrial and rail transportation center in North Korea. Not since the **MISSOURI** bombarded Chongjin in November 1950 had a battleship operated that far north, just 48 miles from the Russian border. Aboard the **IOWA,** they nervously watched the radar as Russian planes took off, but the Soviets never got closer than 20 miles, nor did they interfere with the attack.

It was a well coordinated attack between carrier air strikes and the bombardment of the battleship which delivered 213 tons of munitions before the shelling was complete.

Following an air-sea bombardment of Chongjin on 25 May, the **IOWA** steamed south to Songjin, where on 27 May she fired 98 16-inch rounds, closing tunnels and seriously damaging area bridges. Before being relieved for replenishment on 1 June, she conducted gun strikes on islands in the harbor of Wonsan.

Throughout June, the **IOWA** made gunstrikes on Mayang-do, Tanchon, Chongjin, Chodo-Sokto and the ports of Hungnam and Wonsan. In July and August she was involved in similar operations along the bombline, striking the Wonsan, Songjin, Hungnam and Kojo areas.

On 20 August 1952, the **IOWA** rendezvoused with the destroyer **THOMPSON** that had been struck by the guns at Songjin. Three men aboard the **THOMPSON** had been killed and ten wounded. The **IOWA** sent her doctor to the stricken ship and then took aboard the casualties by highline. As the **THOMPSON** proceeded to safety, the **IOWA** turned its guns on the Songjin position that had hit the destroyer.

During gunstrikes in the Wonsan area on 23 September, General Mark Clark, U.S. Army, Commander-in-Chief of the United Nations Forces joined Vice Admiral Briscoe aboard the **IOWA.** She continued on patrol of North Korean waters firing more than twice the amount she'd fired during World War II.

The **IOWA** served as flagship of the 7th Fleet until 17 October 1952 when she returned to Norfolk for an overhaul followed by training operations in the Caribbean.

In July 1953, **IOWA** took part in operation "Mariner," a major NATO exercise in Northern Europe, serving as flagship of the 2nd Fleet. In 1954 and again in 1955, the **IOWA** visited the Mediterranean becoming the first battleship regularly assigned to the Commander of the 6th Fleet.

Following a midshipman training cruise in June 1955, the **IOWA** entered Norfolk for a 4-month overhaul. Following her refit, she engaged intermittently in training cruises and operational exercises until January 1957 when she returned for duty to the Mediterranean and the 6th Fleet. On

13 June 1957, the **IOWA** took part in the International Naval Review off Hampton Roads, Virginia. After her participation in NATO's Operation "Strikeback" in the North Atlantic, the **IOWA** spent a brief time in Norfolk and then sailed for the Philadelphia Naval Shipyard and decommissioning on 24 February 1958. She had earned 11 battle stars for her service in World War II and Korea.

Her career was not at an end however. In 1981, the Secretary of the Navy decided that the **IOWA** was needed again, and on 1 September 1982, she was towed from Philadelphia to New Orleans and Avondale Shipyard, Inc. for modernization and reactivation. There, hull repairs were made and obsolete equipment was removed. On 30 January 1983 **IOWA** was moved to the Ingalls Shipbuilding and Drydock Co. of Pascagoula, Mississippi for completion of her modernization and reactivation.

Sometimes working 110 hours a week, shipyard workers and **IOWA** crewmen finished the reworking of the battleship in record time. She was ready for recommissioning on 28 April 1984 ahead of schedule and within cost estimates. On 30 April, she was again at sea, on her way to Autec Range for Naval Gun Fire Support (NGFS) training.

Following two weeks of Refresher Training in Guantanamo Bay, Cuba, the **IOWA** arrived off Vieques Island 21 May where NGFS qualifications were run for both the 16-inch and 5-inch batteries. She obtained the third highest score of the year at Vieques.

The **IOWA** departed for Caracas, Venezuela on 19 June 1984. Enroute, she conducted a variety of systems checks and gunnery exercises for her 5-inch and 16-inch batteries using the FAST target. Other areas of training included Harpoon, Tomahawk, Link 11, SAR response, Rainform and Tac-

*This photo, taken in July 1986, shows the clean lines of the **IOWA**'s modernization. The clutter of the many 20 mm and 40 mm mounts about the decks is gone but amidships they have been replaced with missile batteries.*

Another view, taken moments later, shows the same clean lines from another perspective. Note the flight deck on the stern and the UNREP (Underway Replenishment) kingpost to starboard just forward of Turret III.

tical Information Command and Control System (TICCS). The first Radi-osconde launched from the **IOWA** reached a height of 60,000 feet.

Along the way, the **IOWA** made brief stops at several Venezuelan ports as well as ports in Columbia, Jamaica and the Virgin Islands, continuing Naval presence operations to underscore U.S. support for friendly states of Central America and the Caribbean. As part of her mission, the **IOWA** participated in a variety of joint exercises, provided medical and industrial assistance on several occasions and hosted many tours, briefings, dinners and other state ceremonies.

By mid-July, the **IOWA** was again off Vieques Island, this time for illuminated and coordinated 5-inch and 16-inch gunnery exercises and a 16-inch surface gunnery exercise against the **SEPTAR** Hulk and long range 16-inch accuracy tests.

The **IOWA** finished out the month of July with visits to Martinique and Barbados before joining her Battleship SAG task group for operations en-route to and through the Panama Canal. On 8 August she was underway to begin Pacific Coast operations with **USS CONYNGHAM** in company. She embarked two U.S. Army UH-1 Helos which two days later took part in exercises in support of a visit by the Army Chief of Staff. The Helos were again launched on 12 August when medical and dental assistance was needed in Guatemala.

On 13 August, the **IOWA** conducted a successful **SAR** communications drill with the **USS CONYNGHAM** and the Rescue Coordination Center at Howard Air Force Base. The next day, again with the **USS**

CONYNGHAM, the **IOWA** was engaged in surveillance of 13 miles of Nicaraguan coast in conjunction with embassy contingency communication exercises. Throughout the rest of the month of August, the **IOWA** continued her Nicaraguan surveillance while carrying out a number of civic action projects providing medical, dental and industrial assistance to Guatemala and El Salvador.

On 26 August 1984, the **IOWA** completed her surveillance of Nicaragua and returned to Balboa, Panama for her trip back through the Canal. From Panama, she headed north to Port Everglades, Florida and from there to Norfolk, arriving 17 September 1984. A month later, the **IOWA** made a week-long visit to the port of New York and there entertained dignitaries and members of the press. She was inport to Norfolk until 1 November when she left on a southern transit to the Puerto Rican Operations area for **COMPTUEX 1-85. COMPTUEX** was concluded with her return to Norfolk 20 November 1984.

The year ended with numerous inport drills, Christmas ceremonies and the Christmas standdown with the **IOWA** moored at Norfolk's pier 11.

Early January 1985 was spent in preparations for sea trials at mid-month. This was the **IOWA's** first Tiger Cruise since her commissioning in April 1984. Following a standdown in early February, the **IOWA** was underway for deployment in Central America.

Inport time in Panama was spent by officers of the **IOWA,** the **KING** and the **TICONDEROGA** in the planning of tactical techniques and developing and refining support strategies for the Battleship Surface Action

*The **IOWA** fires a broadside during gunnery exercises in August 1984. One of the 16-inch projectiles can be seen in flight on the left. Note the effects of the blast on the water immediately adjacent to the ship.*

A Tomahawk BGM-109 cruise missile is launched to starboard on 2 August 1986. The TLAM-C test firing was made on the Eglin Air Force Base range.

Group (BBSAG). Moving on to Costa Rica and Honduras, the **IOWA** completed a number of civic action and humanitarian projects fulfilling her mission as a peaceful presence in Central American waters.

While in the Western Caribbean, the BBSAG conducted encounter exercises with other naval ships involving long-range plotting and tracking, evaluation of surface and air contacts, and improving the flow of information between the units of the BBSAG. The overall purpose of this particular round of exercises was to integrate the tactical advantages of the Aegis cruiser with the strategic advantages of the Battleship Surface Action Group.

By the end of February, the **IOWA** was enroute to Norfolk for Battle Force integrated training phase #1 and post shakedown availability (PSA)training. She had a brief period at Yorktown for an ammunition offload at the Naval Weapons Station there before moving to the Norfolk Naval Shipyard in Portsmouth preparatory to going to drydock on 26 April.

Throughout her drydock period, PSA continued as well as a variety of exercises and preparations for **Ocean Safari 85** to take place at the end

of August. Upon leaving drydock on 31 July, she moved to Whiskey Anchorage in Hampton Roads to load gun ammunition and demonstate her Tomahawk Handling System prior to 10 days of sea trials and an ammunition onload at the Naval Weapons Station at Yorktown.

Also in August, the **IOWA's** Marine Detachment was rated the best in the Atlantic Fleet and on the 22nd, the **IOWA** received the prestigious Battenberg Cup Award as the best all-around ship in the Atlantic Fleet for 1984.

The **IOWA** got underway 27 August for **Ocean Safari.** Her mission as a part of BBSAG in **Ocean Safari** operations was to provide protection for a convoy of supply ships enroute from Boston to Northern Europe.

Ocean Safari operations carried the **IOWA** northward across the Arctic Circle to rendezvous with the **USS AMERICA** Battle Group in mid-September. Her transit continued toward the southwest approaches to the English Channel in company with NATO Task Group 407.7. The operation ended on 20 September and the **IOWA** proceeded through the English Channel to LeHavre, France, and then to Copenhagen and Aarhus, Den-

A Harpoon RGM-84 missile is launched to port on 20 April 1986. The anti-ship cruise missile was launched during Fleet Exercise 2-86. The missile has not completely exited the launcher in this photo.

mark, and Oslo, Norway which ended 12 October when the **IOWA** got underway for **Baltic Operations (BALTOPS) 85** in the Baltic Sea.

*Shown here as the principal ship of an independent surface action group, the **IOWA** steams in company with the **UNDERWOOD** (FFG 36) ahead, **COMTE DE GRASSE** (DD 974) to port, **CONOLLY** (DD 979) to starboard and **TICONDEROGA** (CG 47) astern.*

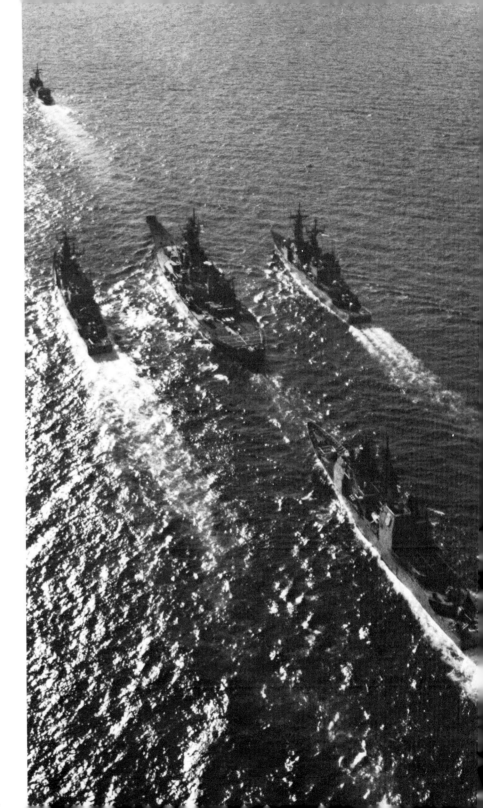

At 1212 hours on 14 December 1986, the **IOWA** fired round number 1,000 of 16-inch ammunition since her recommissioning in 1984. *Above center: Looking on as round number 1,000 is selected are Captain Larry Seaquist, Commanding Officer, GMG 1 Mortensen, turret captain and GMCM Hill, master chief gunner. Above left: Another view of round number 1,000 with Captain Seaquist, Chief Gunner's Mate Smith, and the turret crew. The projectile is a 1,900 pound HC with a MK 29 PDF. Above right: Round number 1,000 comes up into the loading tray from the shell hoist. Note the rotating action of the* tray. *Below right: The projectile has been rammed and the propellant is being loaded in the tray. A reduced charge of 305 pounds of D840 SPDN was used. Note the elevator car of the powder hoist, how the door to the hoist opens down and the propellant is rolled across into the tray. Below left: The firing keys were closed by FCC Fears and round number 1,000 was on its way. Below center: Round number 1,000 was fired from the right gun of Turret II and micro-seconds later the left gun fired round number 1,001. The rounds impacted at 16,000 yards.*

The *TICONDEROGA* comes alongside the *IOWA* for refueling. During her modernization the *IOWA* was converted to burn standard Navy distillate fuel which is used in all fossil fueled surface ships.

The purpose of this annual exercise was to demonstrate the freedom of the seas in these critical international waters and the commitment of the United States to the defense of Northern Europe. During **BALTOPS 85,** the **IOWA** was part of a U.S. Task Unit conducting multi-lateral exercises with our Allies in the Baltic area. To the multi-national operations in the Baltic Sea, she brought state-of-the-art electronics, anti-surface missiles and electronic warfare capabilities, as well as her massive 16-inch and 5-inch batteries. The final exercise bringing **BALTOPS 85** to an end on 18 October involved the entire group of ships, patrol boats, submarines and aircraft.

With the end of **BALTOPS 85,** the **IOWA** was inport at Kiel, West Germany, hosting 33,680 visitors before she got underway for Norfolk on 26 October. Her transit of the North Atlantic was highlighted by a number of communications, electronic warfare, engineering casualty and maneuvering drills as well as covert transit exercises.

The **IOWA** arrived at the Norfolk Naval Base on 5 November 1985 and began preparations for **INSURV/UMI** and her final contract trials conducted in the Virginia Capes operations area. The year ended with a variety of training courses and drills inport at Norfolk.

In February and March of 1986 the **IOWA** returned to Central American waters, displaying as on previous visits a peaceful presence in support of friendly countries.

The **IOWA** with President Reagan aboard, was the focus of national attention during the July 4th "Liberty Week-end" celebrations in New York Harbor. She carried the President as he reviewed the U.S. and foreign warships assembled in the Hudson River for an International Naval Review.

August 1986 found the **IOWA** underway along the Florida coast and in the Gulf of Mexico. In addition to completing a variety of operational and training exercises the gunnery crews continued to increase their proficiency with the successful firing of the ship's 16-inch and 5-inch guns. Of special

The *IOWA* refuels the *HALYBURTON* (FFG 40) during NATO exercise Ocean Safari '85. Note the fuel lines streamed from her UNREP kingpost to the frigate. UNREP is usually conducted at between 12 to 16 knots depending on sea state and weather conditions.

note was the first test firing of a Tomahawk Cruise missile through the joint efforts of the **IOWA's** missile team and the Patuxent River Naval Air Test Center. The missile was launched successfully from the ship to a target on the Eglin Air Force Base Test Range in Florida's Panhandle.

The **IOWA** departed Norfolk on 17 August for the North Atlantic, operation **Northern Wedding** and eventual port visits to Portsmouth, England and Bremerhaven, West Germany. Naval warfare, communications and gunnery exercises continued underway and the **IOWA** was for some time under surveillance by Soviet ships and aircraft.

In September, the **IOWA** was a participant in operation **Northern Wedding** off the southern coast of Norway. With NATO allies, she took part in battle group tactics, anti-surface warfare and naval gunfire support exercises. During the latter exercise, the **IOWA** fired her 16-inch and 5-inch guns at the British Cape Wrath Gunnery Range on the northern coast of Scotland. She also provided simulated gunfire support for a massive amphibious landing of Dutch, British and American Marines.

The **IOWA's** visit to Portsmouth marked the first visit of a battleship to that port since 1956 and she was toured by over 44,000 visitors. She was also greeted warmly in Bremerhaven and hosted over 28,000 visitors before putting out to sea again on 2 October.

In home waters on 9 December, the **IOWA** was underway for sea trials off the Virginia Capes. Operational tests were scheduled for the new Pioneer RPV system and the first launch, flight and recovery of a Pioneer from the **IOWA** was made on the following day. A number of 16-inch firing runs were made and on 14 December, the **IOWA** fired her 1,000th round of 16-inch ammunition since being recommissioned in 1984. Before returning to Norfolk, the **IOWA** also made various speed runs to evaluate maneuvering and handling of the ship in relatively shallow water.

Between 1987 and her decommissioning on 26 October 1990, the **IOWA** deployed to the North Atlantic, the Indian Ocean, the Persian Gulf, and the Mediterranian, logging over 35,000 statute miles and serving as flagship of the Sixth Fleet.

GENERAL DATA

HULL

Name: United States Ship IOWA
Hull Number: BB 61
Builder: New York Navy Yard
Laid Down: 27 June 1940
Launched: 27 August 1942
Commissioned: 22 February 1943
Displacement: 45,000 tons Standard (1945)
57,540 tons Full Load (1945)
53,900 tons Trial Load (1945)
48,425 tons Standard (1984)
57,500 tons Full Load (1984)

Dimensions: 887'3" Length Overall
860' Waterline Length
108'2" Maximum Beam
4' Frame Spacing - 216 Frames
Draft/Loading: 37'9" @ 57,540 tons
154 tons per inch immersion
Decommissioned: 24 March 1949
Recommissioned: 25 August 1951
Decommissioned: 24 February 1958
Recommissioned: 28 April 1984
Decommissioned: 26 October 1990

Complement:

	Officer	Enlisted
1945	151	2,637
1949	166	2,451
1984	65	1,445

MACHINERY

Boilers: Eight B&W three drum double furnace express type.
Pressure: 565 psi
Temperature: 850 degrees F.
Turbines: Four sets General Electric geared turbines
Reduction: Four sets General Electric double reduction
Shaft HP: 212,000
Shaft RPM: 202
Speed: 33 knots
Generators: Eight ship's service, 450 volt, 3 phase, AC (1,250 KW)
Two emergency diesel (250 KW)
Shafts: Four
Propellers: Two five-bladed, 17'0" inboard
Two four-bladed, 18'3" outboard
Rudders: Two semi-balanced streamlined type - projected area 340 sq. ft. each
Fuel Oil: 8,624 tons
Diesel Oil: 187 tons
Gasoline: 8,588 gallons

ARMOR PROTECTION

Amidships: Main Belt - 12.1" on 0.875 STS inclined 19 degrees
Lower Belt - 12.1" tapered to 1.625" on 0.875 STS inclined 19 degrees
Main Deck - 1.50"
Second Deck - 4.75" + 1.25"
Splinter Deck - 0.625"
Third Deck - 0.625"
Turret: Face Plates - 17.0" + 2.7"
Sides - 9.5"
Back Plates - 12.0"
Roof - 7.25"
Secondary: Mounts - 2.5"
Handling Rooms - 2.5"
Barbette: Top to 2nd Deck - 17.3" - 11.6"
2nd to 3rd Deck - 3"
Below 3rd Deck - 1.5"
Conning Tower: Sides - 17.5"
Roof - 7.25"
Deck - 4"
Tube - 16"

ARMAMENT SUMMARY for USS IOWA (BB 61)

WEAPON	Feb. 1943	July 1943	Apr. 1945	June 1946	Jan. 1947	Apr. 1947	Oct. 1951	Apr. 1955	Apr. 1984
16-inch/50 cal. triple:	9	9	9	9	9	9	9	9	9
5-inch/38 cal. twin: ·	20	20	20	20	20	20	20	20	12
40 mm quad:	15	19	19	19	19	15	15	19	
20 mm single:	60	52	52	52	19	15	15	19	
20 mm twin			8		16	16			
20 mm CIWS									4
RGM-84 Harpoon									16
BGM-109 Tomahawk									32

NOTES:
1. This tabulation was taken from the Armament Summaries of the Bureau of Naval Ordnance, 1943 through 1955 and the current Ship's Allowance List.
2. Actual installation of twin 20 mms in 1945 is uncertain.
3. The ultimate approved anti-aircraft battery from the April 1955 Summary was 16, 3-inch/50 caliber twin mounts.

REPRESENTATIVE MISSILE ROUNDS

Weapon/Desig.		Warhead			Speed (Mach.)		Propellant		Range		Guidance
	Item	Wt (lb.)	Type	MK	Cruise	Attack	Cruise	Boost	Mode	NM	
BGM-109	1	1,000	HE		0.50	0.75	Liquid	Solid	TSAM	470	Active Radar
Tomahawk	2	980	HE		0.50	0.75	Liquid	Solid	TLAM-C	675	TERCOM
	3	293	HE-N		0.50	0.75	Liquid	Solid	TLAM-N	1,500	TERCOM
RGM-84	4	510	HE		0.82	0.87	Liquid	Solid	RBL	64	Active Radar
Harpoon	5	510	HE		0.82	0.87	Liquid	Solid	BOL	85	Active Radar

NOTES: 1. The above information has been compiled from unclassified and published sources.

REPRESENTATIVE SERVICE ROUNDS

Gun/Caliber		Projectiles			Velocity (f/s)[2]	Propellant				Assembly	Maximum Range	
	Item	Wt.(lb.)	Type	MK		Powder	Wt.(lb.)	Charge	Sections		El.	Yards[3]
16''/50	[1]1	2,240	A.P.	5	2,700	SPD	640	Full	6	Stacked	45°	47,000
MK7	2	2,700	A.P.	8	2,500	SPD	660	Full	6	Stacked		42,500
RPM:2	3	2,700	A.P.	8	1,800	SPD/N	420	Target	6	Stacked		24,000
	4	2,700	A.P.	8	1,800	SPD/N/CG	305	Reduced	6	Dumped		
	5	1,900	H.C.	13	2,690	SPD	660	Full	6	Stacked	45°	41,600
	6	1,900	H.C.	13	2,075	SPD/N/CG	305	Reduced	6	Dumped		27,379
	7	1,900	H.C.	13	1,900	SPD	325	Reduced	6	Dumped		
	8	1,900	H.E.	14	2,690	SPD	660	Full	6	Stacked		
	9	1,900	HE/CVT	143[4]	2,690	SPD	660	Full	6	Stacked	[5]	[5]
	10	1,880	ICM	144[4]	2,690	SPD	660	Full	6	Stacked	[5]	[5]
	11	1,900	HE/ET	145[4]	2,690	SPD	660	Full	6	Stacked	[5]	[5]
	12	1,900	ICM	146[4]	2,690	SPD	660	Full	6	Stacked	[5]	[5]

NOTES:
1. The gun was originally designed to use the 2,240 lb. A.P. projectile. The 2,700 lb. projectile was adopted in 1939.
2. Projectiles MK 143, 144, 145 & 146 use a modified MK 13 body.
3. Altered ballistics depending on when/where munitions are dispensed. Impact of projectile body approx. 2,000 yards down range from point where munitions are dispensed.

REPRESENTATIVE SERVICE ROUNDS

Gun/Caliber		Projectiles				Propellant			Maximum Range		Maximum Altitude	
	Item	Wt.(lb.)	Type	MK	Velocity (f/s)	Powder	Wt.(lb.)	Charge	El.	Yards	El.	Feet
5"/38(1)	1	53.3	H.C.	35	2,600	(2)	15.5-17(2)	Full	45°	18,200	85°	37,200
MK 12	2	55.1	A.A.C.	35	2,600	(2)	15.5-17(2)	Full	45°	18,200	85°	37,200
RPM: 15	3	54.3	ILLUM	50	2,600	(2)	15.5-17(2)	Full	45°	(3)	(3)	(3)
	4	54.5	WP	50	2,600	(2)	15.5-17(2)	Full	45°	18,200	(3)	(3)
40mm(4)												
(1.57°/60)	5	1.96	A.P.	81	2,890	SPDN	300 gms.	Full	42°	11,000	90°	22,800
MK 1	6	1.985	A.A.C.	½	2,890	SPDN	300 gms.	Full	42°	11,000	90°	22,800
RPM: 160												
20mm(5)	7	0.269	A.P.-T.	9	2,740	SPDN	27.7 gms.	Full	35°	4,800	90°	10,000
(0.8/70)	8	0.271	H.E.	3	2,740	SPDN	27.7 gms.	Full	35°	4,800	90°	10,000
MK 4	9	0.274	H.E/T.	7	2,740	SPDN	27.7 gm.	Full	35°	4,800	90°	10,000
RPM: 450												
20mm(6)	10	0.156	A.P.	149	3,700	WS-19781	650 gns.	Full	45°	11,750		
CIWS Phalanx												
six-barrel												
RPM: 3,000												

NOTES:
1. There were and are a large number of 5"/38 projectiles available for all purposes. The rounds represented are typical of WWII and current ammunition being used.
2. The types of powder in use for all service rounds listed is SPD, SPDN and SPDF.
3. Altered ballistics depending on when/where illumination or smoke is desired.
4. A.P. penetrates 1.7" max. @ 1,000 yds. Tracer burns out @ 5,000 yds. horizontal, 15,000 ft. vertical.
5. Tracer burns out @ 3,000 yds.
6. Sabot round with sub-caliber heavy metal penetrator of depleted uranium. No other data available.

ARMOR PENETRATION

2,700 lb. MK 8 Projectile @2,425 f/s IV(1)

Armor Class	Range/yards	Angle of Fall°	Striking Velocity f/s	Penetration in inches
Class "A" Vertical	14,600	9.86°	1,682	22"
	21,400	17.52°	1,661	18"
	29,300	29.08°	1,530	14"
	39,200	48.74°	1,583	10"
Class "B" Horizontal	15,250	10.58°	1,839	3"
	23,700	20.59°	1,610	5"
	32,700	34.92°	1,515	8"
	39,250	48.90°	1,583	12"

NOTES:
1. Data from ORD 653(c) using initial velocity of a gun with a liner worn to the average life of the liner.

REINFORCED CONCRETE PENETRATION

Slab Concrete (5,000 psi)

Projectile Type	Range/ yards	Angle of Fall°	Striking Velocity f/s	Thickness in ft. Obliquity 0°	30°
2,700 lb. A.P. MK8 @ 2,500 f/sIV(1)	10,000	6°	2,074	27.5'	20.5'
	20,000	15°	1,740	21.0'	15.5'
	30,000	28°	1,567	18.5'	14.0'
	42,345	53°	1,686	20.0'	15.0'
1,900 lb. H.C. MK13 @ 2,690 f/sIV(1)	10,000	5°	2,083	16.5'	13.0'
	20,000	16°	1,606	12.5'	9.5'
	30,000	32°	1,391	10.5'	8.0'
	41,622	57°	1,552	12.0'	9.5'

NOTES:
1. Data from O.P. 1172 using initial velocity of a gun with a new liner.

This photo was taken 14 January 1987 enroute to Central America where she operated for several weeks. Today, the IOWA continues her mission of maintaining the freedom of the seas and defending the United States and its allies with her awesome firepower.

Just before 1000 on 19 April 1989, while steaming northeast of Puerto Rico during a gunfire support exercise, **USS IOWA** became the victim of one of the greatest peacetime tragedies in U.S. Naval History. From causes unknown, the propellant powder in the middle gun of turret number 2 exploded, killing forty-seven members of the ship's crew. During the legnthy investigations that followed, numerous possible causes were examined and rejected. Media coverage was heavy and at times sensational, particularly after circumstantial evidence began to point toward an intentional act by a crew member. Subsequent findings, however, cast doubt upon that explanation, which the Navy could not sustain. Because relevent physical evidence may have been swept overboard shortly after the event or contaminated during the cleanup operations, it is likely that no final explanation will ever be found, and that the true story of that day's tragedy will forever be shrouded in mystery.